Technology-Based Regional Economic Development

Regional technology-based economic development and the recruitment and retention of talent is a top priority for city regions in the United States and globally. However, policy recommendations from government officials, industry leaders, and academics are often ambiguous or are in conflict. To address these issues, this book deals with the complex intersection of institutional theory and national and regional policy initiatives. It provides an overview of the US and Japanese technology policy development at the national level with case analyses of Austin, Texas, and Tsuruoka, Japan, to identify key regional strategies and processes that have resulted in successful endogenous technology-based business development and job creation. The text offers an innovative analytical perspective to improve our understanding of how successful tech-based regional economic development works in theory and practice. The book's discussion is grounded in important technology paradigm shifts in the United States and Japan from 1970 to 1980 leading to current realities.

To address the complex "Puzzle of Space" conundrum, the authors describe similarities and differences in regional development processes in Austin and Tsuruoka. They present a theoretically-based generalizable model indicating necessary and sufficient conditions linked to the building of new "Small i" institutions at the normative and cognitive levels of analysis in consort with regulative policy and innovation at macro-level "Capital I" institutions. The book clearly explains the relations between institutions and economic growth, an important issue in contemporary economics. The book's conclusions clarify critical success factors for endogenous regional development growth theory and lead to recommendations for policymakers searching for ways to achieve success.

Akio Nishizawa is a Senior Research Fellow of New Industry Creation Hatchery Center (NICHe) and Professor Emeritus at Tohoku University, Sendai, and at Toyo University, Tokyo, Japan.

David V. Gibson is a Senior Research Scientist Emeritus at the IC^2 (Innovation, Creativity and Capital) Institute, the University of Texas, Austin.

Routledge Advances in Regional Economics, Science and Policy

For more information about this series, please visit: www.routledge.com/series/RAIRESP

Technology-Based Regional Economic Development

Institutional Perspectives from the United States and Japan

Akio Nishizawa and David V. Gibson

Routledge
Taylor & Francis Group

LONDON AND NEW YORK

First published 2025
by Routledge
4 Park Square, Milton Park, Abingdon, Oxon OX14 4RN

and by Routledge
605 Third Avenue, New York, NY 10158

Routledge is an imprint of the Taylor & Francis Group, an informa business

© 2025 Akio Nishizawa and David V. Gibson

The right of Akio Nishizawa and David V. Gibson to be identified as authors of this work has been asserted in accordance with sections 77 and 78 of the Copyright, Designs and Patents Act 1988.

Trademark notice: Product or corporate names may be trademarks or registered trademarks, and are used only for identification and explanation without intent to infringe.

British Library Cataloguing-in-Publication Data
A catalogue record for this book is available from the British Library

Library of Congress Cataloging-in-Publication Data
Names: Nishizawa, Akio, 1949- author. | Gibson, David V., author.
Title: Technology-based regional economic development : institutional perspectives from the United States and Japan / Akio Nishizawa and David V. Gibson.
Description: Abingdon, Oxon ; New York, NY : Routledge, 2025. | Series: Routledge advances in regional economics, science and policy | Includes bibliographical references and index.
Identifiers: LCCN 2024025506 (print) | LCCN 2024025507 (ebook) | ISBN 9781032784908 (hardback) | ISBN 9781032784922 (paperback) | ISBN 9781003488149 (ebook)
Subjects: LCSH: Economic development—Government policy—United States. | Economic development—Government policy—Japan. | Regional planning—United States. | Regional planning—Japan. | Technology and state—United States. | Technology and state—Japan.
Classification: LCC HC110.E44 N58 2025 (print) | LCC HC110.E44 (ebook) | DDC 338.952—dc23/eng/20240812
LC record available at https://lccn.loc.gov/2024025506
LC ebook record available at https://lccn.loc.gov/2024025507

ISBN: 978-1-032-78490-8 (hbk)
ISBN: 978-1-032-78492-2 (pbk)
ISBN: 978-1-003-48814-9 (ebk)

DOI: 10.4324/9781003488149

Typeset in Sabon
by codeMantra

Dedicated to:
George Kozmetsky (1917–2003)
Dean of the College and Graduate School of Business
The University of Texas at Austin (1966–1982)
Founding Director, IC² Institute (1977–1994)
and
Yoichi Tomizuka (1931–2018)
Mayor of Tsuruoka City (1991–2009)

Contents

Figures

Tables

About the Authors

Akio Nishizawa is a Senior Research Fellow of the New Industry Creation Hatchery Center (NICHe) and Professor Emeritus at Tohoku University, Sendai, and Toyo University, Tokyo, Japan. After being a doctoral candidate in economics from the Graduate School of Social Sciences at the University of Tsukuba, he joined Nomura Securities-affiliated venture capital (VC) firm, Japan Associated Finance Co. Ltd. (JAFCO), and was involved in the establishment of the Japanese first partnership VC Fund in 1982; served as General Manager of Corporate Planning Department; and worked at the Keiwa College, before becoming a professor at the Graduate School of Economics and Management, TOHOKU University. At TOHOKU University, he established leading systems and organizations for industry-academia collaboration in Japan and published articles and books on Technology Venturing and tech-based endogenous regional economic growth and development (please see: https://researchmap.jp/read0181034?lang=en). Association of University Technology Managers (AUTM) awarded him the "Bayh-Dole Award 2005" for his contributions to the globalization of academia tech transfer. He served President of Japan Academic Society for Ventures and Entrepreneurs (JASVE) from 2016 to 2019.

Dr. David V. Gibson is a Senior Research Scientist Emeritus at the IC² Institute at the University of Texas at Austin (UT Austin; www.ic2.utexas.edu). He received his PhD from Stanford University, Department of Sociology. For more than 25 years, Dr. Gibson's research and publications have focused on the enhancing economic and human development of emerging and developed regions worldwide. He was a Fulbright Scholar at Instituto Superior Tecnico, Lisbon, Portugal (1999–2000) and a Visiting Professor at the Arctic University of the North, Tromsø, Norway (2013–2014). He served as Co-Chair—with Professor Manuel Heitor, Instituto Superior Técnico, Lisboa—of *The International Conference on Technology Policy and Innovation* that held conferences in Macau, China (1997); Lisboa, Portugal (1998); Austin, TX (1999); Curitiba, Brazil (2000); Delft, Netherlands (2001); Kansai, Japan (2002); Monterrey, MX (2003); Lodz, Poland (2005); Santorini, Greece (2006); Stavanger, Norway (2007); New Delhi, India (2008); Porto, Portugal (2009); Bogota, Colombia, (2011); Brno, Czech Republic (2014); Milton Keynes, UK (2015). He has directed and helped conduct regional development projects and studies in North America, South America, Central America, the Caribbean region, Europe, and Asia—working with governments and academia to catalyze and grow regional economic development and shared prosperity. Relevant selections of his past "think and do" research which inform his current thinking and writing include:

- *NASA (Field Center Based) Technology Commercialization Centers: Value-Added Technology Transfer for U.S. Competitive Advantage,* National Aeronautical and Space Administration (NASA), Washington D.C. and American Technology Initiative (AmTech) Menlo Park, Ca., IC² Institute, UT-Austin, January 1993.
- *East Tennessee's 21st Century Jobs Initiative: Creating Wealth for a Sustainable Economy,* Tennessee Resource Valley, U.S. Department of Energy, The University of Tennessee at Knoxville, Lockheed Martin Energy Systems, and Oak Ridge National Laboratory, 1997.
- *Cameron County, US/Matamoros, MX: At The Crossroads, assets and challenges for accelerated regional and binational development,* a CBIRD (Cross Border Institute for Regional Development) project and report, The IC² Institute, The University of Texas at Austin and The University of Texas at Brownsville/Texas Southmost College (2002).
- *Toward Global Security and Sustainability: Key Observations, Challenges, and Recommendations, International Science and Technology Center (ISTC), Moscow, Russia* conducted with an international research team including academic colleagues from the United States, European Union, Japan, South Korea, and the Russian Federation (2002–2003).
- *North American Sustainability Consortium and US-Brazil Sustainability Consortium,* FIPSE Grant with Ball State University, IN; Center for Maximum Potential Building Systems, Austin, TX; Federal Center of Technological Education, PR; Pontificia Universidade Catolica do Rio Grande do Sul, RS; Technology Institute of Parana, PR, 2008–2009.
- *The International Collaboratory for Emerging Technologies (CoLab),* IC² Institute, The University of Texas at Austin including departments of computer science, mathematics, and multimedia sponsored by The Portuguese Foundation for Science and Technology (FCT), in close collaboration with Portuguese universities, research institutions, industrial affiliates, entrepreneurs, and regional governments (www.utaustinportugal.org) (2007–2011).
- Advisor to the Campus Committee on Entrepreneurship and Innovation with the University of West Indies Open Campus (2022–2023).

Recent relevant publications include:

David Gibson and Michael Oden (2019), "The Launch and Evolution of a Technology-based Economy: The Case of Austin Texas," *Growth and Change,* 50(3). Wiley Periodicals, Inc.

Bryan Stephens, J.S. Butler, R. Garg and D. Gibson (2019), "Austin, Boston, Silicon Valley and New York: Case Studies in the Location Choices of Entrepreneurs in Maintaining the Technopolis," *Technological Forecasting and Social Change*, September 2019, Vol. 146, pp. 267–280.

Lene Foss and David V. Gibson (Eds.), *The Entrepreneurial University: Context and Institutional Change*, Routledge Studies in Innovation, Organization, and Technology, 2015.

David Gibson, L. Foss, and R. Hodgson, "Institutional Perspectives in Innovation Ecosystem Development," in Thorsten Kliewe and Tobias Kesting (Eds.) *Modern Concepts of Organizational Marketing*, Springer Gabler, 2014, pp. 61–75.

John S. Butler and David V. Gibson (Eds.), *Global Perspectives on Technology Transfer and Commercialization: Building Innovative Ecosystems*, Northhampton, MA: Edward Elgar Publishing, 2011.

Prologue from Austin, TX

I was introduced to Professor Akio Nishizawa in 1999, when he visited the Innovation, Creativity & Capital (IC²) Institute at the University of Texas at Austin to present a paper at the third *International Conference on Technology Policy and Innovation*. He was interested in Austin's rather rapid emergence as a successful tech-based entrepreneurial economy and understanding the factors that were driving the region's *Technopolis* development. To his credit, he believed Austin might offer insights not found in the more well-known larger and well-studied US technopoles of Silicon Valley (California) and Route 128 (Boston, Massachusetts). I was impressed with Professor Nishizawa's astute questions about Austin, as well as his research and observations on the challenges encountered by Japan in its (largely unsuccessful) efforts to foster regional Technopolis development. Over the years, Akio and I motivated each other to question our assumptions about endogenous tech-based growth and to offer each other suggestions concerning interesting and inciteful relevant literature.

Akio made annual visits to Austin which were enhanced by our continuing web-based discussions. We decided to co-author a book to share our ideas reviewing national technology policy formation and impact in the United States and Japan while focusing on the regional level of analysis with case studies of Austin and Tsuruoka. As the book developed, we realized we needed to strengthen the theoretical grounding of our ideas, so we visited my long-term academic mentor and Dissertation Committee Chair Professor W. Richard Scott at Stanford University to benefit from his insights and to enhance the relevance and importance of institutional theory to our research.

By making cross-cultural comparisons at different levels of analysis, we formulated what we hope are innovative and useful insights on regional tech-based development. We have two main objectives: (1) to make substantive theoretical contributions to the research literature on technology-based business development and (2) to provide useful suggestions and advice for city regions in developed and developing nations to successfully build community and prosperity through tech-based entrepreneurial economies—now there's a vision for the future.

IC² Institute
The University of Texas at Austin
Senior Research Scientist Emeritus
David V. Gibson

Introduction

For over 40 years, government officials, business leaders, and academics worldwide have been offering a variety of theoretical and practical models on how to launch and accelerate endogenous tech-based growth. The idealized models or examples of success have commonly been Silicon Valley, California, and along Route 128 surrounding the City of Boston (Boston R128) in Massachusetts. There are a range of perspectives explaining how each of these regions became exceptionally successful in growing technology-based innovation economies, and we elaborate on some of these reasons in the following pages. However, our main target audience for this book are the many other city regions worldwide that have not achieved their desired objectives in terms of stimulating tech-based economic growth and attracting, growing, and retaining needed talent. We highlight what, we believe, are key barriers or challenges that are common to many of these failed or underwhelming efforts to achieve even modest success in regional wealth and job creation. To explain our reasoning, we describe important national and regional economic policy initiatives and strategies in the United States and Japan beginning in the late 1970s and extending to current realities with a focus on the regional level of analysis.

Helpman (2004, p. ix) in *The Mystery of Economic Growth* noted that, while economists have been studying the economic growth of nations since the days of Adam Smith, the Scottish moral philosopher and political economist, in *The Wealth of Nations* (1776), "the subject has proved elusive and many mysteries remain." North (1990, p. 107) defined the fundamental role of institutions in societies as "the underlying determinant of the long-run performance of economies" but that, without being able to "see, feel, touch, or even measure institutions," there are many contradictory studies on the relation between institutions and economic growth. For example, Acemoglu et al. (2019), after observing the different economic development states of North and South Korea as "A Natural Experiment of History," state that the trajectory of economic growth of these two countries can be attributed to "Inclusive and Extractive Economic Institutions." These researchers contend that "inclusive economic institutions (in South Korea) foster economic activity, productivity growth, and economic prosperity, while extractive economic institutions (in North Korea) fail to do so." They conclude that "the

DOI: 10.4324/9781003488149-1

Korean example provides strong support for the institution hypothesis (but it does not provide direct evidence against geography and culture, because these were held fixed in this comparison)" (2019, p. 574–577).

Since the 1980s, there has been mixed results in the growth and decline of US cities working with or operating under "inclusive economic institutions." Storper (2013) notes that US cities can be divided into growing (Winners) and declining (Losers) and that these differences of US intercity economic growth demonstrate that macro-institutions at the national level alone cannot effectively determine successful regional economic development. Based on his study of US urban economies from 1980 to 2000, Storper (2013) argues that "Small i" institutions, defined as regional mezzo-level institutions, are the critically important difference as they are key to regulating or stimulating economic development more directly than national-level macro-institutions which he categorized as "Capital I" institutions.

Building on Storper's research with the intention of further developing these ideas, at the national level of analysis, we offer a comparative overview of US and Japanese technology growth policy beginning in the 1970s. At the regional level of analysis, starting in the mid-1980s, we compare two city regions—one in the United States and the other in Japan—that succeeded, beyond the expectations of many experts, in growing successful tech-based endogenous economic development. Importantly, our comparative target cities of Austin, Texas, USA, and Tsuruoka, Yamagata, Japan, exemplify important and comparable successful economic growth strategies despite operating under considerably different historical, political, and cultural contexts.

We realize that there is increasing criticism of national and regional policy initiatives focused on regional wealth and job creation as it commonly leads to increased income inequality, gentrification of communities, increased traffic congestion, and environmental challenges that are currently being exacerbated by climate change impacts faced by all, but especially those not usually benefiting from such technology-based economic development and growth (Florida, 2017; Piketty, 2020; Tatsuno, 2022). This book does not address these important and relevant concerns, as our focus is on what we contend is the fundamental importance of regional wealth and job creation. For without viable growth economies regions will have neither the necessary financial resources nor the ability to attract and retain needed talent—resulting in a diminished capacity to address these increasingly important regional and national challenges.

1   Background: Stagflation and New Economic Policy

From the late 1970s and into the early 1980s, saving national economies from severe stagflation was a major and urgent driver of macroeconomic policy in many industrialized countries including the United States, Europe, and Japan, as well as many developing countries. While skyrocketing oil prices were considered the main cause of stagflation, we contend that stagflation was profoundly exacerbated by the global reliance on vertically integrated

"Fordist-style" industry that historically stimulated economic growth, especially during the 1960s, with mass-production and mass-consumption of analogue-based technologies and production. Increasingly, however, national and regional leaders have realized that saving their economies from poor performance required launching and growing knowledge-based high-tech[1] industries rather than trying to resuscitate existing "Fordist-style" industry (Neal, 1999). Accordingly, "Technopolis strategy" was seen by many policy makers as the best hope for economic growth leading to the development of 1,000+ tech parks worldwide beginning in the late 1980s (Tatsuno, 2023).

Over the years, "Technopolis-motivated" policy recommendations have largely been simplistic and often in conflict as researchers and policy makers could not agree on how best to stimulate regional development by launching and growing knowledge-based high-tech industries. And, while there has been increased awareness that there is limited benefit to simply analyzing the pros and cons of macroeconomic policies, there is still considerable controversy in terms of best policy recommendations for city regions. For example, on the one hand, Mazzucato (2014) argues that a state's risk-taking research and development (R&D) investments are crucial to achieve innovation that drives economic growth, and that policies which rely heavily on private companies have not been productive. On the other hand, McCloskey and Mingardi (2020), while agreeing that state support is an important part of the supply chain especially concerning R&D, criticize Mazzucato's policy recommendation of emphasizing state involvement while ignoring the important commercialization activities of entrepreneurial companies.[2]

In her well-received 1994 publication *Regional Advantage: Culture and Competition in Silicon Valley and Route 128*, Saxenian emphasizes the importance of Silicon Valley's unique culture of decentralization and collective learning when compared to Boston; however, she does not provide a viable theoretical lens to help us understand the "Puzzle of Space." In fact, her "regional advantage" argument seems to contradict the reality of Boston's emergence as an important "Life Science Cluster." Powell et al., (2012) emphasize this complexity by noting that the United States had over ten areas with the conditions capable of building life science clusters, but only three areas came to dominate: San Francisco, Boston, and San Diego.

Storper (2013, pp. 97, 227) notes that, given the challenges of explaining regional economic development, it is the area of institutions that is perhaps the most complex yet least explored topic in that "the regional institutions that matter most are largely hidden from the naked eye." Building on Storper (2013), we emphasize the importance of "Small i" institutions, which we define as the core of "Local Context" and we emphasize the importance of "robust actors" to institutionalizing processes required for successful tech-based economic development. We also emphasize the important connection between "formal" and "informal" constraints of institutions as proposed by North (2003) as being centrally important in the relationship between "Capital I" and "Small i" institutions. In this discussion, we refer to the relationship between the "Iron Cage" theory and the concept of "Isomorphism" as proposed by P. DiMaggio and W. Powell (1983) concerning institutional change proposed by R. Scott (2014), please refer to Table 0.1 for an overview of these issues.

The Organization Field Model proposed by Scott (2014, p. 237) emphasizes the changeability of institutions through clarification of institutionalization processes and suggests that the challenge for contemporary institutional studies lies in institutionalizing processes rather than structural analysis. Accordingly, while referencing the Organization Field Model, we focus analysis on "New Small i" institution building processes that enable R&D-driven tech-based endogenous regional economic development. An important theoretical and practical question is how "New Small i" institutions at normative and cultural-cognitive levels of analysis can be implemented successfully to supplement "New Capital I" institutions that are formulated and implemented by policies backed by laws and regulations (Table 0.2). In order to provide useful answers to these questions, we reference Scott's Organization Field Model to provide a theoretical basis for demonstrating how "robust actors" and "influencers" at normative and cultural/cognitive levels of analysis help build and sustain "New Small i" institutions that enable the reduction and sharing of risks faced by technology startups.[3]

Table 0.1 Classification of Institutions by Selected Researchers

	Macro: National Level	*Mezzo: Regional/ Urban Level*	*Theoretical Points*
DiMaggio and Powell (1983)	"Iron Cage" with isomorphic pressure	"Iron Cage" with isomorphic pressure	Institutional change is complex and difficult.
North (1990)	Formal constraints	Informal constraints	Informal constraints are defined by codes of conduct, norms of behavior, and conventions, which are (1) extensions, elaborations, and modifications of formal constraints; (2) socially sanctioned norms of behavior; and (3) internally enforced standards of conduct.
Storper (2013)	"Capital I" institutions	"Small i" institutions	"Small I" institutions play important roles in differentiating urban economic performances at the regional level.
Scott (2014)	Regulative pillar	Normative pillar and cultural cognitive pillar	The pillars of institutions may resist changing processes. Collective rationality is critically important for institutionalization.

Sources: DiMaggio and Powell (1983), North (1990), Storper (2013), and Scott (2014).

Table 0.2 Three Pillars of Institutions

	Regulative	*Normative*	*Cultural-Cognitive*
Basis of compliance	*Expedience*	*Social obligation*	*Taken-for-grantedness* *Shared understanding*
Basis of order	Regulative rules	Binding expectations	Constitutive schema
Mechanisms	Coercive	Normative	Mimetic
Logic	Instrumentality	Appropriateness	Orthodoxy
Indicators	Rules Laws Sanctions	Certification accreditation	Common beliefs Shared logics of action Isomorphism
Affect	Fear Guilt/innocence	Shame/honor	Certainty/confusion
Basis of legitimacy	Legally sanctioned	Morally governed	Comprehensible Recognizable Culturally supported

Source: Scott (2014, p. 60).

We explore these questions through comparative research on our target cities, Austin, Texas, and Tsuruoka, Japan. We describe how both city regions built "New Small i" institutions to enable their tech-based economic policy agendas in concert with "New Capital I" institutions. Referencing the Technopolis Wheel Framework (TWF) (Smilor et al., 1989; Gibson & Rogers, 1994), we note that both these regions exhibited strong similarities in the building "New Small i" institutions despite their considerably different historical, cultural, political, and economic contexts. Finally, we present a generalizable model showing the necessary and sufficient condition linked to institutional theory and the building of "New Small i" institutions referring to Scott's Organization Field Model at normative and cognitive levels of analysis in consort with regulative change by "New Capital I" institutions.

2 Outline of This Book

2.1 Chapter 1: "New Capital I" Institutions and New Technology Policies in the United States and Japan

Chapter 1 identifies and provides an overview of important US macro-policy initiatives and actions in the late 1970s and early 1980s, designed to transform the national economy from analogue-based large-scale manufacturing to an R&D-driven digital-tech-based knowledge economy to help save the United States from stagflation. We describe the importance of "New Capital I" institutions that were introduced by US "Industrial Innovation Policy"[4] under the Carter and Reagan administrations—formulated and implemented to overcome stagflation as we also review important and conflicting policy initiatives under "neoliberalism" during the Reagan administration. Additionally, we clarify the content and background of the Japanese "Natural Experiment of History," pursued in the late 1990s, in which the national government worked to duplicate Silicon Valley-type high-tech clusters by introducing "Cloning Silicon Valley Policy" that was modeled on "the Industrial Innovation Policy" adopted in the United States in the late 1970s.

2.2   Chapter 2: "New Small i" Institutions of the World's First Technopolis and Key Reasons for Japan's Failed Technopolis Policy

To clarify the background formulation of Technopolis policy in the United States, we review studies on the formation of Boston R128 as the first and one of the largest technopoles in the world (Preer, 1992). Even during severe stagflation of the late 1970s, Boston was able to achieve considerable economic growth led by the minicomputer industry with an agglomeration of related companies located around the circular highway R128. Boston's R128 and California's Silicon Valley have long been regarded as preeminent models of successful tech-based endogenous regional economic growth. In discussing both these regions, we introduce the significance and function of "New Small i" as well as "New Capital I" institutions as having an important impact on launching endogenous tech-based economic growth. In both regions, we focus on the key role played by "robust actors" fostering the commercialization of Department of Defense's (DOD) military-based R&D through university tech-based startups. We also explain how Japan's failed Technopolis Policy and "New Capital I" institution building initiatives at the regulative level failed to stimulate regional economic development as policy makers did not fully understand the importance of regionally based "New Small i" institution building processes.

2.3   Chapter 3: Technology Venturing and Theoretical Modeling for "New Capital I" and "New Small i" Institutions

In Chapter 3, we explore three important topics of our United States-Japan comparative analysis focused on tech-based growth: (1) why institutions need to adapt or change to foster tech-based growth, (2) what important roles "New Capital I" and "New Small i" institutions play in these change processes, and (3) what are important institutionalizing processes for sustainability. These three underpinning issues provide key concepts to clarify and discuss the similarities revealed by our comparative analysis of our targeted US and Japanese city regions. Scott's (2014) Organization Field Model alerted us to the possibility of defining a theory-backed practical model for building "New Small i" institutions that enable regions to launch and sustain successful endogenous tech-based regional economic growth. While research has long emphasized the importance "robust actors" as being indispensable for building "New Small i" institutions, their specific roles and functions have not been fully clarified. To address this issue, we identify the activities of "robust actors" in building "New Small i" institutions in keeping with the Organization Field Model as a theoretical lens for our United States-Japan comparative case analyses in Chapter 4.

2.4 Chapter 4: Case Studies: Austin, Texas, USA, and Tsuruoka, Yamagata, Japan

Chapter 4 focuses on the case studies of Austin, Texas, USA, and Tsuruoka, Yamagata, Japan. Both cities have been successful in launching endogenous tech-based economic growth in city regions that historically had minimal experience as R&D-based innovation economies. In both cases, we take the "New Small i" institution building process out of the "black box" while referring to Scott's Organization Field Model to provide guiding insights for institution building processes. The case of Austin has a broad perspective and discusses a more total regional transformation toward a globally competitive tech-based economy. Tsuruoka's case is more focused on the establishment of an entrepreneurial university and incubator with an in-depth analysis of the launch of a company startup in the bio-tech industry. While we note these differences, we also highlight similar characteristics and strategies of both regions, such as building "New Small i" institutions important to a unifying regional vision. We identify "influencers" in addition to "robust actors" as a necessary and sufficient condition for building "New Small i" institutions that enabled Austin and Tsuruoka to launch and grow endogenous tech-based regional economic growth as we get inside the "black box" of regional context.

2.5 Chapter 5: Conclusion: Important Conditions for Successful Endogenous Tech-Based Economic Development

It is our intention to provide useful, theoretically sound, and practical advice concerning "New Capital I" and "New Small i" institution building processes based on Scott's Organization Field Model while clarifying important observations at regulative, normative, and cognitive-cultural levels of analysis. We conclude that, while we present a limited empirical analysis of two city regions (one in Japan and the other in the United States), we are able to help clarify—at different levels of analysis—the important role of institutions and human actors in endogenous tech-based growth which we believe is an enduring, if not increasingly important, issue in modern economies of both developed and developing nations. Furthermore, we suggest that the underlying philosophy of innovative institution-based activity at national and regional levels of analysis advocated in this publication may also help provide a useful orientation to addressing important worldwide challenges—such as increasing income inequality, gentrification of communities, unbridled and life threatening immigration, and environmental challenges and climate change impact —faced by all societies but especially by those marginalized as a result of technology-based economic development and growth (Florida, 2017; Piketty, 2020; Tatsuno, 2022).

Notes

1 High-tech industries are defined as having a sales R&D ratio of more than 4%, according to the Organization for Economic Cooperation and Development (OECD), including aerospace, computers and office machinery, electronic communication, and pharmaceuticals (Sandven et al., 2005).
2 Neither of these perspectives seems to credit the major technology paradigm shift to digital technology that was occurring in the 1980s and resulted in a crisis of regional imbalance (Atkinson et al., 2019). Furthermore, McCloskey & Mingardi (2020) are anachronistic in their criticism of Mazzucato's theory by looking to "the Great Enrichment" that brought about the industrial revolution as a basis for their argument.
3 Currently in the popular press and media, the term "influencer" refers to an individual who commands considerable influence on an audience of followers through social media and by disseminating information on popular trends or ideas. Decades earlier, Smilor et al. (1989) and Gibson & Rogers (1994) defined "influencers" as "regional actors" who had exceptional ability to network across public/private sectors to foster community-wide activities and visions such as to accelerate regional technology-based economic development. Importantly, this characterization of "influencer" was before the internet and before the wide-spread use of transformative social media.
4 Link and Cunningham defined "Industrial Innovation Policy" as "Technology Policy," which they noted had its origins in the innovation creation measures recommended by Vannevar Bush, US Director of the Office of Scientific Research and Development, report to President Roosevelt "Science the Endless Frontier," July 1945. (Link & Cunningham, 2021).

References

Acemoglu, D., D. Laibson & J. List (2019). *Economics*, 2nd Edition. London, UK: Peason Education Inc.

Atkinson, R. D., M. Muro & J. Whiton (2019). *The Case for Growth Centers: How to Spread Tech Innovation across America*. Washington, DC: Brookings ITIF.

DiMaggio, P. J. & W. W. Powell (1983). "The Iron Cage Revisited: Institutional Isomorphism and Collective Rationality in Organizational Fields," *American Sociological Review*, 48(2), 147–160.

Florida, R. (2017). *The New Urban Crisis: How Our Cities Are Increasing Inequality, Deepening Segregation, and Failing the Middle Class-and What We Can Do about It*. New York: Basic Books.

Gibson, D. V. & E. M. Rogers (1994). *R & D Collaboration on Trial: The Microelectronics and Computer Technology Corporation*. Brighton, MA: Harvard Business School Press.

Helpman, E. (2004). *The Mystery of Economic Growth*. Cambridge, MA: Harvard University Press.

Link, A. N. & J. A. Cunningham (2021). *Advanced Introduction to Technology Policy*. Northampton, MA: Edward Elgar.

Mazzucato, M. (2014). *The Entrepreneurial State: Debunking Public vs. Private Sector Myths*. London, UK: Anthem Press.

McCloskey, D. N. & A. Mingardi (2020). *The Myth of the Entrepreneurial State*. Great Barrington, MA: American Institute for Economic Research.

Neal, R. (1999). "History and Current Legislative Perspective on SBIR Program," pp. 41–45, in W. Charles (Ed.), *The Small Business Innovation Research Program: Challenges and Opportunities*. Washington, DC: The National Academies Press.

North, D. C. (1990). *Institutions, Institutional Change and Economic Performance*. Cambridge, UK: Cambridge University Press.

Piketty, T. (2020). *Capital and Ideology*. Cambridge, MA: Harvard University Press, 2020.

Powell, W. W., K. Packalen & K. Whittington (2012). "Organizational and Institutional Genesis," pp. 434–465, in J. F. Padgett & W. W. Powell (Eds.), *The Emergence of Organizations and Markets*. Princeton, NJ: Princeton University Press.

Preer, R. W. (1992). *The Emergence of Technopolis: Knowledge-Intensive Technologies and Regional Development*. Westport, CT: Praeger.

Sandven, T., et al. (2005). "Structural Change, Growth and Innovation," pp. 31–59, in H. Hirsch-Kreinsen, et al. (Eds.), *Low-tech Innovation in the Knowledge Economy*. Frankfurt: Peter Lang Publishing.

Saxenian, A. (1994). *Regional Advantage: Culture and Competition in Silicon Valley and Route 128*. Cambridge, MA: Harvard University Press.

Scott, W. R. (2014). *Institutions and Organizations: Ideas, Interests, and Identities*, 4th Edition. Los Angeles, CA: SAGE.

Smilor, R. W., D. V. Gibson & G. Kozmetsky (1989). "Creating the Technopolis: High-Technology Development in Austin, Texas," *Journal of Business Venturing*, 4(1), 49–67, Elsevier.

Storper, M. (2013). *Keys to the City: How Economics, Institutions, Social Interaction, and Politics Shape Development*. Princeton, NJ: Princeton University Press.

Tatsuno, S. (2022). *The Gaiapolis Strategy: Designing Bionic Cities for Pandemic, Energy and Climate Resilience in the Coming Bio Renaissance*. Independently Published, 2022.

Tatsuno, S. (2023). Personal communication with David. V. Gibson and A. Nishizawa, via email dated June 24 and July 7.

1 "New Capital I" Institutions and New Technology Policies in the United States and Japan

1 US Industrial Innovation Policy in the late 1970s and early 1980s

The building of "New Capital I" institutions in the United States began as macroeconomic policy to save the US economy from stagflation in the late 1970s when facing severe social and economic turmoil. While the global oil crisis and skyrocketing oil prices caused by the Middle East War were commonly said to be a direct cause of stagflation, weakened US industrial competitiveness made it considerably worse as reflected in "the US Misery Index" (Cohen et al., 2014).[1] The industrial competitiveness of US-produced steel, shipbuilding, household electric appliances, and automobile manufacturing was diminishing while manufacturing capabilities in Europe and Japan were rebounding and strengthening following World War II. Even in high-tech industries such as semiconductors and computers, Japan had increased its competition with high-quality production, benefitting from public-private research and development (R&D) consortiums organized at the initiative of Ministry of International Trade and Industry (MITI). Reeling from intense Japanese industrial competition, the Carter administration put the highest priority on recovering from stagflation and increasing US industrial competitiveness by enacting policies to revitalize innovation in leading high-tech industries with the potential to compete effectively with Japan (Turner, 2006).

In May 1978, the Carter administration established the "Domestic Policy Review on Industrial Innovation (DPR)" to investigate concrete measures that would strengthen US industrial innovation capabilities. The DPR performed multifaceted investigations for 18 months with 250 participants from 28 federal agencies and 150 representatives from industry, academia, and government. In the end, the DPR proposed several new macro-policies to enable US industry to create disruptive innovations, which were seen as laying the seeds for US high-tech industries to regain global competitiveness (Wolff, 1980). Accepting the DPR's proposals, on October 31, 1979, President Carter sent *Industrial Innovation Initiatives Message to the Congress on Administration Actions and Proposals*,[2] recommending the following nine initiatives:

DOI: 10.4324/9781003488149-2

1 Enhancing the transfer of technical information
2 Increasing technical information
3 Improving the patent system
4 Clarifying antitrust policy
5 Fostering the development of smaller innovative firms
6 Improving federal procurement
7 Improving the regulatory system
8 Facilitating labor/management adjustments for innovation
9 Maintaining a supportive attitude toward innovations

Importantly, these nine initiatives were strongly linked to a technology paradigm shift from physically based analogue to knowledge-based digital technologies which motivated changing US economic structure. Existing dominant industries such as steel, shipbuilding, household electric appliances, and automobile manufacturing were founded on capital-intensive physically based analogue technologies performed by vertically integrated big business which had led US economic development and prosperity in the early half of the 20th century. However, in the late 1970s, these industries were experiencing shrinking sales in the face of intense Japanese and European competitors. Rather than attempting to rejuvenate the US economy through trying to resuscitate these formerly dominant industries (symbolized as "Fordist-style" economy by auto manufacturing centers in Detroit, Michigan), the nine DPR initiatives proposed by the Carter administration aimed to proliferate the high-tech models of Boston R128 and Silicon Valley, which were realizing stunning economic growth even during existing stagflation (Leslie, 1993; Neal, 1999; Turner, 2006).

It is significant that the economies of Boston R128 and Silicon Valley were catalyzed by disruptive innovations and the commercialization of breakthrough digital technologies which had emerged from collaborative R&D under the "Military-Industrial-Academic Complex" initiated by the Department of Defense (DOD) just after World War II (Fabrizio & Mowery, 2005). However, a major concern was that many large corporations found "Use-inspired basic research" results to be too embryonic and far from commercialization. Unlike analog technologies that could be adjusted to technological needs through physical adjustments, digital technologies required binary code programming and research to analyze technological needs and enable commercialization. It became clear that tech-based startups[3] could fill this critical role (Leslie, 1993).[4]

It was also realized that tech-based startups were not able to scale and grow as profitable high-growth firms through limited military markets alone, and when DOD was the sole customer, it was not feasible to reduce technical risks and develop commercial applications. Leslie (1993) emphasized that DOD-reliant tech-based startups needed to expand their markets from military to civilian use, in order to significantly strengthen the competitiveness of US high-tech industries. At the time, not only in computer and related technological areas but in other high-tech industries, the United States was losing its competitive edge due to Japan's rapid economic expansion (Stevens, 2004). In short, it was important to expand collaborative R&D in nonmilitary fields (Brunton, 1991). Indeed, federal government officials had been working to strengthen US high-tech industries' competitiveness by enhancing disruptive innovation capabilities, while similar measures introduced by the DOD enabled tech-based startups to commercialize breakthrough technologies as they emerged from academia-industry collaborative R&D. The Institutional Patent Agreement (IPA), introduced by N. Latker, Deputy General Counsel at the Department of Health Education and Welfare (HEW) in 1968, allowed universities to take title to inventions that resulted from their research under federally funded grants and to conduct collaborative applied research between universities and industry (Stevens, 2004).

In 1973, the National Science Foundation (NSF) followed HEW in supporting the IPA; in addition, in 1977, R. Tibbetts at the NSF led the establishment of a new program, "the forerunner of the Small Business Innovation Research (SBIR) program" to enable tech-based startups to commercialize federally funded research results in industries outside "medical and weapon areas" (Wessner, 1999). However, these programs were not embedded as federal-level institutions due to (1) considerable public/private criticism of transferring federal R&D results to the private sector, (2) challenges in directing funding and procurement to small businesses, and (3) strong oppositions from universities concerning possible reduction of federal basic research funding.

Importantly, the Carter administration encouraged Congress to give legal and formal basis to the nine DPR initiatives. Congress ultimately enacted the Industrial Innovation Policy that was formulated and implemented under the Carter and Reagan administrations with the goal of rescuing the US economy from stagflation by fostering the creation of high-tech industries based on digital technologies (National Academy of Engineering, 1980). Yet, the federal government's Industrial Innovation Policy alone would prove to be insufficient to form high-tech industries by focusing on creating disruptive innovations commercialized by tech-based startups. New laws and regulations formulated and implemented by Congress toward the end of the 1970s and early 1980s were considered essential in building new institutions that would provide necessary incentives and new frameworks to enhance industrial innovation through tech-based growth and to facilitate the success and growth of tech-based startups. Table 1.1 provides a list of the historical development of major US Industrial Innovation Policy initiatives from the 1970s to the 1980s, and these initiatives are described in the following sections.

Table 1.1 Historical Development of Major "Industrial Innovation Policy" in the United States from the early 1970s to the late 1980s

Year	Policy	Effect
1973	NSF establishes Industry-University Cooperative Research Centers (IUCRC)	Accelerates the impact of basic research through close relationships between industry innovators, world-class academic teams, and government leaders.
1977	NSF SBIR	Helps small innovative firms to commercialize NSF-funded research results emerging from universities. This initiated the Small Business Innovation Development Act of 1982 and the SBIR program.
1978	Revenue Act	Reduces maximum rate on Capital Gains taxes from 49.5% to 28.0%
1979	ERISA reformation	Lifts ban on investment funds to VC Limited Partnership (LPS) funds.
1980	Bayh-Dole Act (formerly the Patent & Trademark Act Amendments)	Permits small businesses and nonprofit organizations to (1) retain title to inventions they created while working on a government-sponsored program, (2) apply for and receive patents on those inventions, and (3) pursue options to commercialize those discoveries.
	• Small Business Investment Incentive Act	• Excludes VC from the Investment Company Act of 1940.
	• Stevenson-Wydler Technology Innovation Act	• Allows government owned/operated laboratories to enter into cooperative R&D agreements (CRADAs). Previously, technology transfer was not a part of the mission of most federal agencies.
1981	Economic Recovery Tax Act	Reduces maximum rate on capital gains taxes from 28.0% to 20%.
1982	SBIR and Small Business Technology Transfer (STTR)	Expands NSF SBIR across all federal agencies. SBIR offers competitive awards to stimulate technological innovation among small private-sector businesses while enabling government agencies to work with emerging high-technology businesses. STTR's purpose is "to bridge the gap between the performance of basic science and commercialization of resulting innovations." Usually referenced as SBIR/STTR, they are promoted together as America's Seed Fund.
	• Regulation D	• Allows capital to be raised through the sale of equity or debt securities without the need to register those securities with the SEC.

(Continued)

Table 1.1 (Continued)

Year	Policy	Effect
1984	NCRA	Reduces the potential antitrust liabilities for various types of joint ventures involving R&D, production, or standards development in order to encourage their formation and operation.
1986	Federal Technology Transfer Act (FTTA)	Expands on the Stevenson-Wydler Act of 1980. Improves access to federal laboratories by nonfederal organizations. Allows government inventors to patent their technologies and receive a share of licensed patents royalties. Goal: to put federally funded technology to use in real-world applications.
1987	Executive Order 12591	Holds federal labs accountable by ensuring they assist universities and the private sector through transferring technical knowledge. Emphasizes the government's commitment to technology transfer and urges the use of agreements to the limits permitted by law.

Source: Authors.

2   An Overview of "New US Capital I" Institutions

Storper (2013) introduced the idea of categorizing national-level formal institutions built by laws and regulations as "Capital I"[5] institutions. We extend this categorization to include "New Capital I" reflecting the institutional changes inspired by US Industrial Innovation Policy which was implemented by a series of federal laws and regulations toward the end of the1970s and early 1980s (Figure 1.1).

To clarify the features of "New Capital I" institutions, we classify them, as follows, into three fields: (1) *university tech-transfer institutions*, (2) *facilitating private equity markets*, and (3) *tech-based startups supporting institutions.*

1 University Tech-Transfer Institutions

The Bayh-Dole Act gave research universities the right to own and profit from patents emerging from their federally funded R&D activities using university-based Offices of Technology Licensing (OTL). The Bayh-Dole Act initiated a noticeable shift from anti-patent to pro-patent incentives for academia-industry technology transfer (Bremer, 2002). In addition, University-Industry Research Centers (UIRC) established by the NSF in 1976 were expanded in the 1980s to allow research universities to collaborate their R&D activities with both governmental agencies

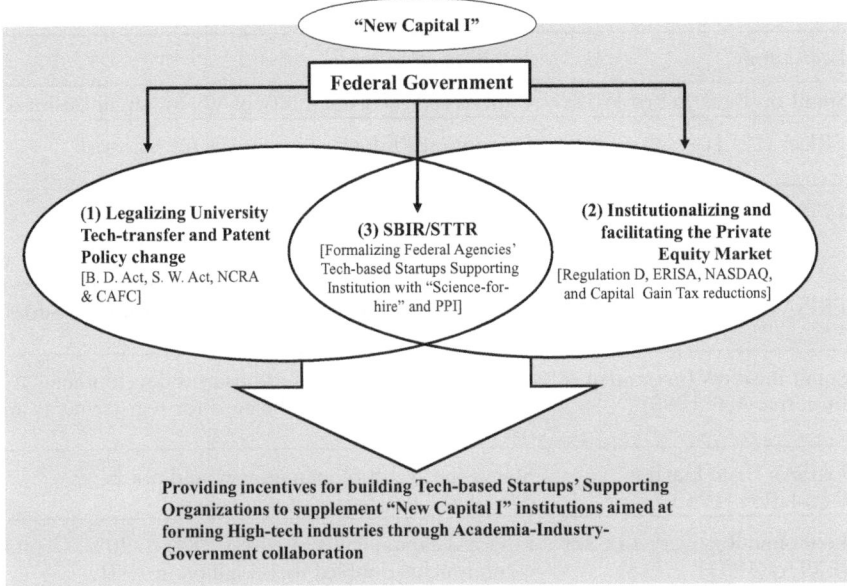

Figure 1.1 The US "New Capital I" Institutional Policies, the late 1970s to the early 1980s

and/or for-profit private companies (Berman, 2012). The 1984 National Cooperative Research Act (NCRA) exempted academia-industry collaborative R&D consortiums from the most serious financial penalties of antitrust laws through the concept of "pre-competitive R&D" (Gibson & Rogers, 1994; Stevens, 2004).

Each of these initiatives provided strong incentives for research universities to introduce "Use-inspired basic research" as accepted research activities including tech-transfer to private industrial corporations under the new academia-industry relations which had been developed at Massachusetts Institute of Technology (MIT) and Stanford. After acknowledging the significance of newly introduced university tech-transfer institutions in the early 1980s, Etzkowitz (1996, p. 127) contends that "schools such as MIT and Stanford which had been anomalies within the US academic system now became the models for other universities to emulate."

2 Facilitating Private Equity Markets (PEMs)

Another important policy shift was to make investing in tech-based startups easier through deregulation, adding incentives to stimulate venture capital (VC) investments, allowing pension funds' investments, and decreasing the capital gain tax rate (Table 1.2).

The Employment Retirement Income Security Act (ERISA) reformation of 1979 lifted the ban on investments from pension funds to VC Limited Partner funds, and the Small Business Investment Incentive Act of 1980

Table 1.2 Legislative Impact on Venture Capital (VC) Investment

Legislation	VC Impact
Small Business Act of 1958	• Increased the availability of VC for small business.
ERISA (1974)	Discouraged fiduciary incentives for high-risk investments.
1978 Revenue Act	Provided capital gains tax incentives for equity investments. Capital committed increased by 556 million from the previous year.
ERISA's "Prudent Man" Rule	Clarified investment guidelines for pension investors to allow for higher risk investments.
Small Business Investment Incentive Act (1980)	Redefined venture firms as business development companies, eliminating the need for registering as an investment advisor.
ERISA's "Safe Harbor" Regulation (1980)	Stated that venture managers would not be considered fiduciaries of plan assets.
Economic Recovery Tax Act (ERTA) (1981)	Lowered capital gains rate from 28% to 20%. Capital commitments doubled to 1.3 billion in 1981.
Tax Reform Act of 1986	Reduced incentive for long-term capital gains.

Source: Bygrave and Timmons (1992, p. 24).

excluded VC from the Investment Company Act of 1940 which severely restricted VCs' management activities in relation to Limited Partner funds. At the same time, capital gain tax rates were reduced as an incentive to promote VC investment.[6] Under these new laws and deregulations, "the sleepy, cottage [VC] industry of the 1970s was transformed into a vibrant, at times frenetic, occasionally myopic, and dynamic market for private risk and equity capital in the 1980s" (Bygrave & Timmons, 1995, p. 27). Regulation D introduced by the US Securities and Exchange Commission (SEC) in 1982 also allowed "accredited investors" to be business angels (Mason & Harrison, 1996), and the reformation and expanding of the National Association of Securities Dealers Automated Quotations (NASDAQ) in 1982 established a more vigorous Initial Public Offering (IPO) market especially for tech-based startups (National Association of Securities Dealers, 1987). These reforms played important roles in expanding VC investment activities and, significantly, creating new equity financing institutions categorized as PEMs in the United States.

These laws and regulations made VCs and PEMs "New Capital I" institutions that were important to funding tech-based startups in 1980s.[7] However, while the expansion of PEM aimed to support tech-based startups as "smaller innovative firms," it contributed more to the deconstruction of existing companies than to the actual support of tech-based startups in the 1980s, since the return on investment (ROI) for tech-based startups took longer than traditional businesses, while leveraged buyouts (LBOs) and other forms of financing to deconstruct existing companies could yield high investment returns quickly (Fenn et al., 1995).

3 Tech-Based Startups Supporting Institutions

SBIR initiatives empowered federal agencies to support tech-based startups as the creators of disruptive innovations. Federal programs such as "Science-for-Hire" and "Public Procurement for Innovation (PPI)," which had been originally implemented by DOD for military technological R&D, encouraged the practical application of digital-based breakthrough technologies after World War II. The SBIR enabled tech-based startups to create disruptive innovations, which helped transform and expand military technology R&D funding and commercializing schemes (organized by DOD) to other federal governmental agencies. Because of SBIR program successes, this "temporal" legislation received repeated extensions and ultimately became institutionalized as a key supporting measure for realizing disruptive innovation through tech-based startups.

Under SBIR programs, federal agencies were able to establish contractual hires and to collaborate with topnotch regional research universities to perform specific R&D as their normal business activities. Servo (2005) contends that "without federally funded Science-for-Hire programs, many small technology firms would not survive as private sector investors prefer to wait until technology and market risks are reduced before investing their funds" (Servo, 2005, p. 24). SBIR programs also played a critical role as Blank and Dorf's (2012) definition of "earlyvangelist"[8] (or the first customer), purchasing prototypes through PPI while extending and utilizing R&D capabilities of tech-based startups toward realizing disruptive innovations. SBIR awards showed a 12.8% annualized growth rate from 1983 to 2018 which played a particularly vital role in underpinning hi-tech industries when the IT bubble burst, coupled with a drastic decrease in VC startup and seed investments. When VC investment in early-stage technological development flagged, SBIR funding played an increasingly important role in providing "earlyvangelist" tech-based startups investment (Wessner, 2008). Figure 1.2 shows the steady growth of SBIR awards from 1983 to 2018 and the up and down swings of VC seed funding during this same period of time.

While the Carter administration took important initiatives for building "New Capital I" institutions, major positive economic results under these institutions were largely realized during the Reagan administration and into the 1990s (Turner, 2006). It took almost ten years to enable "New Capital I" institutions to evoke nation-wide economic growth in the United States based on knowledge-based digital technologies. "New Capital I" institutions needed time (1) to achieve results through the transformation of regional flagship research universities into entrepreneurial universities as best symbolized by MIT and Stanford, (2) for the growth of firms like Digital Equipment

[in millions of dollars]

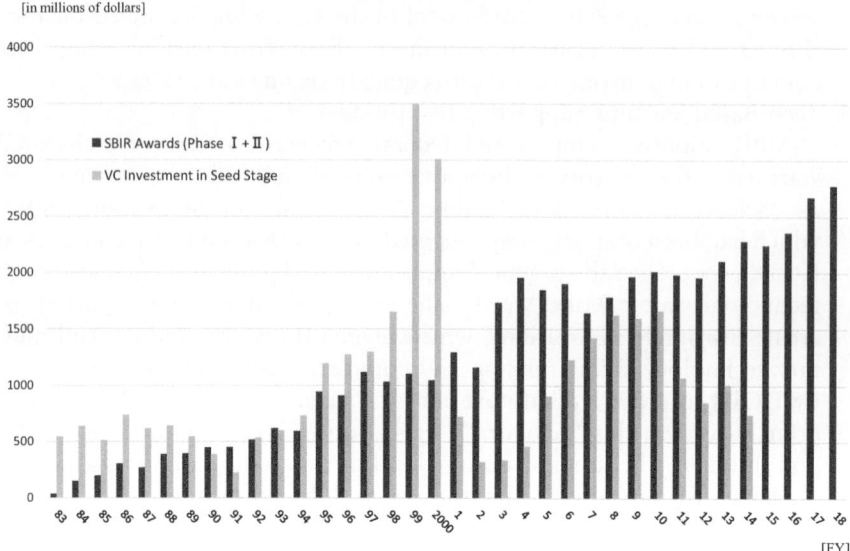

Figure 1.2 Value of SBIR Awards and VC Seed Investment

Source: SBIR Awards; *SBIR/STTR Annual Reports,* Each Year, Office of Technology, US SBA, VC Seed; FY 1983–1984 data *from NVCA Year Book 2009,* 1985–2014 from *NVCA Yearbook 2015.* However, VC Investments data by Stage appeared in NVCA Year Book had been discontinued from 2016

Corporation (DEC) and Intel as anchor tenants coming from tech-based startups, and (3) for the creation and expansion of PEMs including venture capitalists. All these efforts as elaborated below played critical roles in the formation of high-tech industries in Boston R128 and Silicon Valley.

3　Essential Role of the US "New Capital I" Institutions

In the late 1970s, "New Capital I" institutions initially proposed by the Carter administration and implemented by both the Carter and Reagan administrations provided new frameworks for collaborative R&D between academia and industry. These collaborative R&D centers were essential for creating diverse high-tech knowledge-based technological industries which, in turn, were necessary for the transition from analogue mass production to digitally based economies. To facilitate disruptive innovations emerging from commercializing digital technologies, "Existing Capital I" institutions accommodated "New Capital I" institutions where cross-sector R&D collaborations could facilitate the commercialization of breakthrough inventions. Etzkowitz (1996) categorized these changes as the "convergence of Military and Civilian R&D" that would also transform "the Military-Industrial-Academic Complex" to the "Triple Helix Model" of academia-industry-government collaboration for tech-based economic development (Etzkowitz & Leydes-dorff, 2000; Etzkowitz, 2002).

While it could be said that "the Military-Industrial-Academic Complex" was essential in forming high-tech industries in Boston R128 and Silicon Valley, those high-tech industrial clusters alone were not sufficient to revive the US economy from stagflation. Accordingly, the proliferation of high-tech industrial clusters composed of high-growth tech-based startups commercializing digital technologies encouraged Academia-Industry-Government (AIG) collaboration with the expectation that new military technologies could be converted to civilian use (Leslie, 1993; Cohen & Delong, 2016). On the one hand, the Industrial Innovation Policy was not expected to intervene directly in civilian sector R&D, but rather facilitate AIG collaborative R&D by providing incentives for research universities to voluntarily introduce use-inspired research and tech-transfer as an important mission. On the other hand, the Industrial Innovation Policy's contribution to building "New Capital I" institutions was criticized and opposed by many main-stream economists and academics (Stein, 1994).

Establishing and expanding PEMs and introducing SBIR programs were important policies to strengthen the US industrial innovation capabilities through building "New Capital I" institutions instead of directly intervening in the private sector or academic R&D processes. However, an important result of the Industrial Innovation Policy is that it became a historical trigger to build "New Capital I" institutions while providing a signaling effect for regional institutional change. Industrial Innovation Policy could be defined as an "indirect industrial policy" to build "New Capital I" institutions enabling (1) incentives for universities to pursue use-inspired basic research and facilitate collaborative R&D with private corporations and government agencies, (2) the creation and expansion of PEM to facilitate equity investments in tech-based startups and thus promote commercializing breakthrough technologies emerging from entrepreneurial universities, and (3) federal support systems to enable tech-based startups to grow through creating disruptive innovations (Etzkowitz, 2002). In short, these newly built "Capital I" macro-institutions were important to rescuing the US economy from stagflation by helping to transform US industry from Fordist-style analogue-tech-based mass manufacturing to a digital-tech-based knowledge economy.

4   Reagan Administration's Contradicting Policies

Reaganomics is often defined as supporting policies to rescue the US economy from stagflation by revitalizing market mechanisms, emphasizing small government, and deregulation based on "neoliberalism" or "market fundamentalism." *Reaganomics* attempted to replace Keynesian demand control policy with monetary control policy aimed at accelerating corporate investments by using incentives such as capital gains tax rate reduction, while drastically cutting welfare budgets and weakening the collective bargaining power of labor unions.[9] However, in reality, the Reagan administration simultaneously implemented contradictory policies by expanding interventions in strengthening US industrial innovation capabilities that had been initiated by the Carter administration.[10] Indeed, the Reagan administration implemented SBIR and NCRA in contradiction to "neoliberalism" or "market fundamentalism" enabling federal agencies to support basic and applied research activities implemented through academia-industry collaborative R&D. Under SBIR, federal agencies could also act as the first purchaser, or "earlyvangelist," for tech-based startups and thereby enhance their capacity to develop disruptive innovations capacities. At the same time, the NCRA softened the effects of antitrust laws in contradiction to "market fundamentalism."

"Existing Capital I" institutions had facilitated "Fordist-style" economic growth and stability through creating a large middle-income class that benefitted from wage negotiations between big businesses and big labor unions installed during the New Deal era to save the US economy from the Great Depression of 1929 (Lemann, 2019). In the early 1980s under *Reaganomics*, two contradictory types of activities were taking place which (1) offered less support for industries under "Existing Capital I" institutions based on physical-based analogue and big business economies and (2) offered more support for tech-based startups under "New Capital I" institutions seen as key to creating high-tech industry through commercializing knowledge-based digital technologies. This technological revolution from physical-based analogue to knowledge-based digital-tech economies underpinned the contradicting policies adopted by the Reagan administration. While the Reagan administration tried to downplay the implementation of macro-policies proposed by the Carter administration, many of the *Reaganomics* policies that enabled the transformation of the US economy were initially proposed by the Carter administration.[11]

It is important to remember that the "Existing Capital I" institutions enabled the considerable economic prosperity labeled the Golden 60s. However, due to increased and severe foreign competition, existing US institutions and structures were not up to the task of mitigating stagflation. While stagflation[12] could be seen as the historical trigger for building "New Capital I" institutions in the late 1970s, it also led to deconstruction of big businesses with vertically integrated organizations, weakening the bargaining power of big labor unions and the regulatory reforms to transform the Keynesian demand control policy, which had been effective under "Existing Capital I" institutions. Furthermore, the revitalization of market mechanisms, which focused on monetarism policy, led to the accelerated destruction of big businesses by exhibiting poor business performance through investments from Private Equity (PE) funds that were activated by institutional investors such as pension funds. This deconstruction of "Existing Capital I" institutions by the Reagan administration enabled new organizations and entities to be reconstituted as "New Capital I" institutions.

Importantly, "New Capital I" institutions were prerequisite to creating high-tech industries and reviving entrepreneurship with tech-based start-ups through the liquidity of labor markets, facilitating tech-transfer under academia-industry R&D collaborations, and enabling existing companies to work with tech-based startups.[13] On the one hand, it is important to realize that "New Capital I" institutions were at times assimilated into "Existing Capital I" institutions through "Isomorphism" (DiMaggio & Powell, 1983). On the other hand, it could be argued that *Reaganomics* inhibited this "isomorphism."[14] Ultimately, however, "New Capital I" institutions played a critical role in saving the US economy from stagflation by encouraging regions to build new support institutions and to expand high-tech industries' development as exhibited in Boston R128 and Silicon Valley.

Significantly, "New Capital I" institutions alone were not sufficient for the United States to develop and grow high-tech clusters like Boston R128 and Silicon Valley. For example, while the University of Pennsylvania, Caltech, and the University of California also received considerable military funding from DOD, these institutions and their surrounding regions were not successful in fostering regional high-tech industry clusters. We contend that these universities did not have the necessary supportive regional context or regional "*genius*"—which we categorize as "New Small i" institutions—necessary to duplicate the success of Boston R128 and Silicon Valley (Storper, 2013).

5   Introducing "Cloning Silicon Valley Policy" in Japan

Toward the end of the1980s, at the peak of its bubble economy, Japan enjoyed the second largest Gross Domestic Product (GDP) in the world. However, it failed to keep that position into 2010 as mainland China became the world's second largest economy based on GDP. While the Japanese government tried to rejuvenate its economy by stimulating the creation of knowledge-based industries such as Information and Communications Technology (ICT) and biotech, these efforts spawned mixed results without spurring an effective national economic recovery. In short, into 2020 Japan continued its struggle to escape the long economic slump losing industrial competitiveness (Figure 1.3) and income stagnation (Figure 1.4) resulted in the "Lost Three Decades." Indeed, Japan suffered further economic setbacks in 2022–2023 as a result of the COVID-19 pandemic.

Japan's biggest economic policy issue during the early 1990s was to liquidate nonperforming financial assets accumulated during the bubble era and to restore soundness to financial institutions. Toward the end of 1990s, when the disposal of nonperforming financial assets had been almost completed, a new economic revitalization plan was formulated and implemented. The Japanese government—especially the MITI, which changed its name to the Ministry of Economy, Trade and Industry (METI) after the reorganization of Central Government's ministries and agencies in 2001—introduced the Japanese version of "Cloning Silicon Valley Policy" hoping to revitalize its

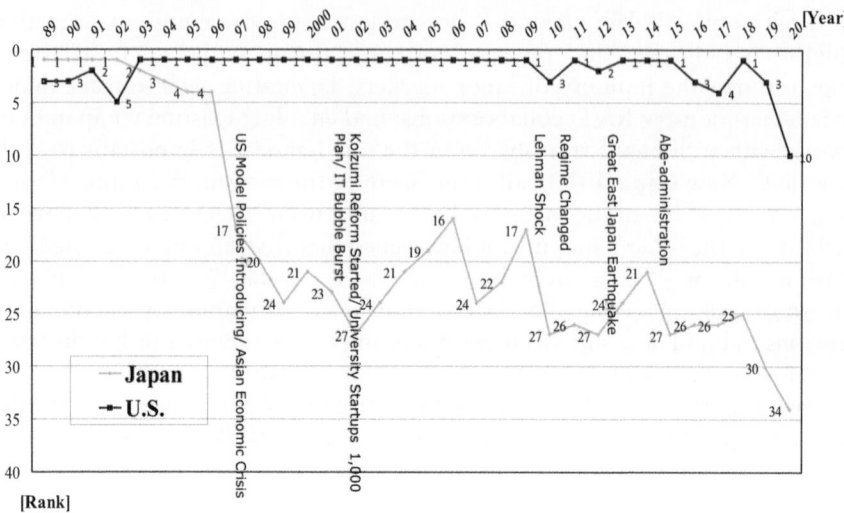

Figure 1.3 Japan's Lost Industrial Competitiveness: 1989–2020

Source: Prepared by author from *IMD Annual Survey Report*

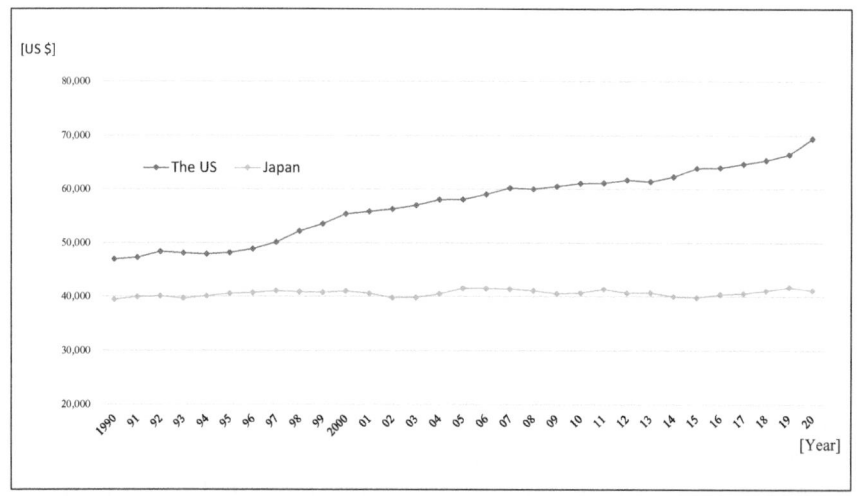

Figure 1.4 Japan's Income Stagnation: 1900–1920

Source: Prepared by the author from OECD Economic Data

national economy from long deflationary stagnation caused by the burst of its bubble economy. Japan had lost its industrial competitiveness during three decades of economic slump, and the nation's digitization, biotech, and drug-design capabilities proved ineffective for its economic rejuvenation.[15] Why has Japan's weakened industrial competitiveness persisted without signs of recovery, despite having such strong industrial competitiveness in the late 1980s? Our research seeks to answer this question and, specifically, why the Japanese version of "Cloning Silicon Valley" introduced toward the end of 1990s did not stimulate such a recovery.

Through its "Cloning Silicon Valley Policies," it is no exaggeration to say that MITI tried to introduce the type of "New Capital I" institutions that were established under US Industrial Innovation Policy and implemented toward the end of the 1970s and the early 1980s.[16] As shown in Figure 1.5, it was clear that by introducing "Cloning Silicon Valley Policies," the government expected to save Japan's economy from a prolonged recession by duplicating Silicon Valley-type "New Capital I" institutions and high-tech industry clusters in specific regions throughout Japan.

Under "New Capital I" institutions, the Japanese government sought to form high-tech industrial clusters through commercializing disruptive innovations coming out of its universities' advanced research through tech-based startups. Japan's "Cloning Silicon Valley Policies" were implemented under the Koizumi administration (2001–2006) in an attempt to reduce the central government's intervention with the intergovernmental relationship reformation between the central and regional governments— which had formed the foundation of the postwar economy in addition to postal reformation, financial liberalization, and labor market deregulation. In 1993, the "New Capital I" institutions introduced by Japan's "Cloning Silicon Valley Policies" attempted to formally institutionalize academia-industry technology transfer systems, PEMs to stimulate VC and private equity investments, and SBIR-type programs to strengthen Japanese industrial competitiveness.

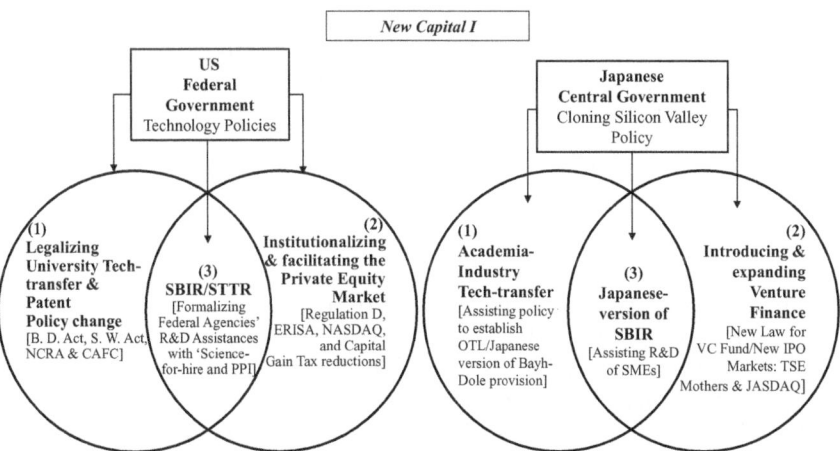

Figure 1.5 Similarities of the "New Capital I" Macro-Policies between the United States and Japan

Source: Authors

However, in retrospect, it is clear that these "New Capital I" institutions conflicted with existing norms and culture of established Japanese institutions and organizations, while not producing the expected technology-based economic growth. Indeed, introducing academia-industry technology transfer through newly established Technology Licensing Organization (TLO), Japan's version of the American OTL, led to significant conflict among "star professors" in the engineering departments at the old Imperial Universities (Japan's major research universities) as these universities had, over time, established informal intellectual property transfer mechanisms with private companies, especially with big businesses, and they had enjoyed a relatively good track record of efficient patent utilization (Kneller, 1999).

Similarly, the Japanese version of the US Limited Partnership VC fund was expected to facilitate and expand VC investment in tech-based startups. However, at the time, Japanese VCs were focused on "growth-equity capital" functions with investing in medium-sized companies rather than tech-based startups (Nishizawa, 2009). The Japanese version of SBIR also failed to move from its "Value for Money" principle of public procurement to "Value for Innovation" and became commonly used as subsidy support for the R&D of existing SMEs without introducing "Science-for-Hire" and PPI supporting systems.

The US federal government's Industrial Innovation Policy was defined as "indirect industrial policy" and a "Feeder's Position" building "New Capital I" institutions aimed at providing incentives for inducing bottom-up region-led efforts to build supporting organizations for tech-based startups.[17] In contrast to the US "Feeder's Position," the Japanese government took a "Leader's Position" that attempted to establish new regional institutions through a top-down approach to create the supporting organizations for university startups.

METI implemented an "Industrial Cluster Policy" in addition to a "Cloning Silicon Valley Policy" to enable academia-industry collaborations to create disruptive innovations and for university tech-based startups to form regional high-tech industrial clusters centered around strong research universities. The "Industrial Cluster Policy" targeted areas considered to have high potential to form Silicon Valley-type high-tech clusters. METI introduced incentives to enable selected regions to grow tech-based startups emerging from government-academia-industry R&D collaboration. Matching grants from METI headquarters were competitively awarded, based on METI-designed selection criteria—which we suggest were overly complex and included unrealistic objectives for "Regional Clustering Organizations"—as depicted in Figure 1.6.[18] Importantly, regions would receive MITI funding and other support based on their compliance with such frameworks.

The "Industrial Cluster Policy" required regional governments to establish collaborative academia-industry R&D organizations. University tech-based startups were expected to play a critical role in creating high-tech industries in the fields of Information and Communication Technology (ICT), biotech, life sciences, healthcare, energy, and environment[19] by developing disruptive innovations in cooperation with METI's nine regional offices across Japan. METI proposed to establish at least 1,000 university startups within three years. Ultimately, Japan's "Cloning Silicon Valley Policies" in combination with its "Industrial Cluster Policy" were unsuccessful.

In addition to a prolonged recession, Japan was facing severe cost competition with rapidly developing Asian countries, especially mainland China. Japanese companies were forced to cut labor costs by replacing "regular" workers with "nonregular" workers, made possible through the Koizumi administration's labor market deregulation. However, severe depression caused by "the Lehman shock" in 2008 led to massive layoffs of both regular and nonregular workers. These considerable challenges impacted political opinion and the Democratic Party of Japan (DPJ) came to power in 2009, claiming that the "Cloning Silicon Valley" policies of the Koizumi administration, failed due to incompatibility with Japan's existing institutions and resulted in an increasing disparity between Japan's rich and poor. Accordingly, the DPJ ended major parts of "Industrial Cluster Policy" as it shifted away from economic growth policies toward economic distribution policies.

Japan's "Cloning Silicon Valley Policies" were not totally eradicated even under the DPJ administration. For example, as the newly introduced academia-industry technology transfer systems were expanded to include academia-industry R&D collaboration, joint research activities increased

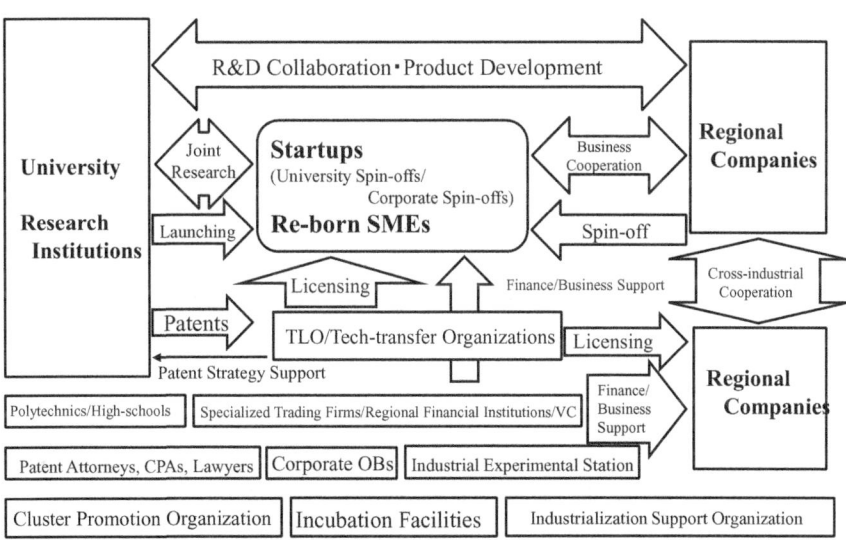

Figure 1.6 Regional Clustering Organizations and Strategies Expected under METI's Cluster Policy

Source: Industrial Cluster Study Group, *Report on Industrial Cluster*, METI Industrial Cluster Study Group, May, 2005, p. 13

between academia and for-profit companies, which stimulated change in Japanese research universities (Yoshioka-Kobayashi & Takahashi, 2022). While in 2022, Japan's VC investment remained relatively low (1.3% of the United States), in recent years VC disbursement amounts, the amount of Limited Partner funds, and the amount of money invested in startup and early-stage companies has increased to over 70% of the total amount of VC investment (VEC, 2022). Furthermore, the Japanese version of SBIR has also undergone reforms that allow for PPI in 2021 (*Nihon Keizai Shinbun*, 2021).

In summary, while parts of Japan's "Cloning Silicon Valley Policies" were institutionalized under severe political turmoil, "Cloning Silicon Valley Policies" in combination with its "Industrial Cluster Policy" failed to create significant high-tech industrial clusters in Japan. We conclude that a major reason for the resulting failure was the design and implementation of top-down policies—without grasping the necessary institutional change needed at the regional level for successful high-tech industry formation and the use of "inducements" that would encourage and support regionally based endogenous tech-based industrial development (Eisinger, 1988). However, national and regional decentralization policies[20] pursued under the Koizumi administration, coupled with the deregulation of national and local government agencies, was an important start to enabling regions to pursue locally inspired economic revitalization policies. The case of Tsuruoka presented in Chapter 4 is an example of the positive impact of these new Japanese economic and political contexts, starting in the late 1990s.

Notes

1 The Misery Index was originally published by A. Okun, researcher at the Brookings Institution, as the "Economic Discomfort Index (EDI)" in 1970 became popularized as the "Misery Index" in 1976, when Democratic presidential candidate Jimmy Carter referenced the EDI as the "Misery Index." Carter strongly criticized his incumbent opponent (Gerald Ford), saying that anyone realizing a Misery Index as high as 12.5 should not be reelected as president. Ironically, when Carter ran for his second term, he lost face when Republican presidential candidate Ronald Reagan criticized his administration based on the same Misery Index which exceeded the highest number of the Ford administration (Cohen et al., 2014).

2 President Carter's message on industrial innovation was an epoch-making proposal outlining macro-institutional change required to realize a technological paradigm shift from physically based analogue to knowledge-based technologies (Link & Cunningham, 2021).

3 There was strong concern that small businesses would be unable to induce disruptive innovation because they were thought to have quite low R&D capabilities. However, university startups proved to be quite successful in commercializing the R&D results that emerged from "the Military-Industrial-Academic Complex," in lieu of small businesses in the traditional sense (Turner, 2006). As the military techno-market steadily expanded its R&D activities, defense procurements emerged that helped lower the initial cost for entering new sectors and enabling university startups to commercialize newly developed digital R&D results more readily. Such tech-based startups spinning out from MIT and Stanford through

their growth and agglomeration established Boston R128 and Silicon Valley as leading technology centers (Leslie, 1993). It can be concluded that small businesses, as mentioned in the DPR's nine categories, were embodied by tech-based startups that commercialized breakthrough technologies as they emerged from universities, research institutes, and corporate R&D centers and ultimately became the high-growth potential tech-based firms by innovative entrepreneurial activities categorized as Schumpeter's Mark I (Freeman, 1982). In fact, most disruptive innovations of the 20th century were realized by innovative entrepreneurs who commercialized breakthrough technologies through tech-based startups (Baumol, 2010).

4 The technological breakthroughs that V. Bush noted concerning World War II depended on the knowledge of different fields of science. Stokes proposed "Use-inspired basic research" in addition to "Pure basic research," which aims to explore basic principles (Stokes, 1997, p. 18). H. Etzkowitz defined "Use-inspired basic research" as "Entrepreneurial Science" and proposed the Triple Helix Model in which industry, academia, and government collaborate to enable the creation of disruptive innovation (Etzkowitz, 2002). In fact, the digital technology development represented by the SAGE (Semi-Automatic Ground Environment) system was conducted at MIT's Lincoln Laboratory under the "Military-Industrial-Academic Complex" (Leslie, 1993).

5 We introduce the categories of "Capital I" institutions as the formal constraints of the people built by laws and regulations, and "Small i" institutions as the informal constraints for regional inhabitants embedded with normative and cultural/cognitive levels to help explain differences of cities' economic growth in the same country and same regulatory environment (Storper, 2013). The differences of formal and informal constraints were categorized by D. North (1990). While we appreciate these institutional categories, we differentiate "Existing" from "New" to clarify existing economic structures and policy from newly emerging entities which we posit as key to contributing to regional tech-based economic growth.

6 While no tax reform proposals were included in the nine categories, some DPR members insisted tax incentives were essential for expanding VC investment in tech-based startups that had played important roles in building Boston R128 and Silicon Valley (Wolff, 1980).

7 PEMs, "New Capital I" institutions, played critical roles not only facilitating business angel, VC, and similar investments in tech-based startups but also deconstructing and reorganizing vertically integrated big businesses through buyouts, mergers, and acquisitions. Actually, the amount of non-venture investment Limited Partnership Funds was more than double that of venture investment, because non-venture Limited Partnership Funds could result in higher performances from leveraged buyout aiming at restructuring existing companies, especially big businesses (Fenn et al., 1995).

8 Often disruptive innovations were unable to develop a market base for commercial success, and this lack of demand ultimately led to failure (Christensen, 1997). The disruptive innovations which emerged from commercializing digital technology depended on defense demands as the first users, or "earlyvangelists," who were critical to nurturing tech-based startups (Blank & Dorf, 2012). Therefore, we can conclude that PPI was indeed an important national "earlyvangelist."

9 An important symbolic event was the Reagan administration's forceful intervention in the strike of the Professional Air Traffic Controllers Organization (PATCO) in August 1981 firing all the striking air traffic controllers and hiring replacements. This dramatic intervention significantly weakened the trade union movement.

10 The Reagan administration aimed to revive and strengthen market mechanisms under neoliberalism through deregulation and small government and did not formally adopt measures to foster high-tech industries by the federal government. To the contrary, such policies were not officially recognized by the federal government until the G. Bush administration (Link and Cunningham, 2021). However, the Reagan administration could not neglect the fact that employment and output were sluggish or declining in older American industries—such as steel and automobiles—but rising within certain newer industries, mainly connected with electronics, and output of these newer industries was rising elsewhere, notably in Japan, and so were US imports of these high-tech products" (Stein, 1994).

11 Lemann (2019) described the change in relationship between "Organization" and "Man" to "Institutional Man" at the end of World War II until the 1970s to "Network Man" from the 2000s via "Transaction Man" under Reaganomics in the 1980s. Etzkowitz and Leydesdorff (2000) also proposed an evolution model that goes from the "Statist Model" through the "Laissez-faire Model" to "Tri-lateral Networks and Hybrid Organization" which was defined industry-academia-government collaboration as the Triple Helix (Etzkowitz & Leydesdorff, 2000; Nishizawa, 2011).

12 Through the lens of institutional theory, we can see that the contradictory policies implemented by the Reagan administration might inhibit "New Capital I" from being isomorphic to "Existing Capital I." It has been observed that "Existing Capital I" institutions, legitimized by historic positive effects, could survive alongside competing "New Capital I" through forced "Isomorphism" in organizational fields. "Isomorphism" is the key concept in creating "Iron Cage" institutions (DiMaggio & Powell, 1983). Importantly, the demolishing policies adopted by the Reagan administration enabled "New Capital I" to expand more smoothly and rapidly without isomorphic pressures.

13 According to Chesbrough (2003), International Business Machine Corporation (IBM), a good example of a vertically integrated corporation, transformed its business model by unbundling its corporate organization and value-chain by adopting "Open Innovation."

14 Schumpeter stated that the essential fact of capitalism is that it incessantly revolutionizes the economic structure from within, incessantly destroying the old, while incessantly creating the new in a process he labeled "Creative Destruction" (Schumpeter, 2008). Acemoglu et al. (2019) pointed out that "Creative Destruction" also manifests itself as "Political Creative Destruction" because new economic growth disenfranchises existing stakeholders. Hence, selection by winners and losers through impersonal price competition in the market introduced by Reaganomics is said to be more effective (Storper, 2013, p. 107).

15 On September 1, 2021, Japan established the Japan Digital Agency with the stated mission of helping to reform "the culture of administration in a user-driven manner through digitalization" because "the COVID-19 pandemic highlighted the delay in digitalization of Japan's administration" as cited from the home page of Digital Agency of Japan (URL: www. digital.go.jp).

16 Modeled on the US policies introduced in the late 1970s and early 1980s to tame stagflation, Japan's rescue policies of the late 1990s to correct the nation's long-term deflationary slump were not expected to show results for 20 years. But, we suggest, Japan's most important policy failure was not recognizing the need for "New Small i" institutions.

17 Feld (2012) insisted that the federal government should be devoted to the role of Feeder, not Leader, for the regional startup community to support tech-based startups.

18 This type of slide served as a basis for regional policy makers to create institutions that were aligned with METI's policy goals. In fact, METI funding was implemented through selecting regional institutions based on the extent to which regional policy makers formed organizations that resembled the regional support organizations envisioned by METI. Regional policy makers were required to structure support organization that fulfilled the conditions shown in Figure 1.9. While this approach resulted in uniform implementation of METI's policies across the country, it also suppressed divergent regionally led policies more in-tune with local context.

19 Eighteen projects were selected as candidates for Industrial Clusters including Hokkaido Office (Sapporo City) for IT and biotech; Tohoku Office (Sendai City) for IT; Kanto Office (Saitama City) for IoT and biotech; Chubu Office (Nagoya City) for IoT and biotech; Kinki Office (Osaka City) for biotech, energy, and environment; Chugoku Office (Hiroshima City) for IT, biotech, and environment; Shikoku Office (Takamatsu City) for biotech; Kyushu Office (Fukuoka City) for environment, semiconductors, and biotech; and Okinawa (Naha City) for IT and Environment, proposed by MITI's nine regional offices. Interestingly, the Ministry of Education, Culture, Sports, Science and Technology (MEXT, formerly the Ministry of Education), which initially opposed the use of university functions for METI's economic policy, because of the high-profile nature of this policy situation, competing with METI, initiated the "Knowledge Cluster Initiative" in 2002, to focus on upgrading regional capabilities of academia-industry collaboration and technology transfer businesses of universities. *MEXT Report on Knowledge Cluster Initiative* said, "MEXT selects a region and provides funds to core organizations in order to realize the cluster vision for the local region." MEXT resulted in designating 18 candidates as its "Knowledge Clusters" which were totally overlapping METI's Industrial Clusters projects.

20 As will be seen in Chapter 2, while implementing the Technopolis Policy in the early 1980s, Japan's central government, like the Reagan administration in the United States and the Thatcher administration in the United Kingdom, undertook administrative and fiscal reforms under "deregulation" policy to reduce the involvement of the central government. As part of these efforts in the United Kingdom, the *Local Autonomy Law*, which strictly regulated the relationship between the central government and the prefectural and municipal governments, was amended in 2000 to grant more autonomy to prefectural and municipal governments.

References

Acemoglu, D., D. Laibson & J. List (2019). *Economics*, 2nd Edition. London, UK: Peason Education Inc.

Baumol, W. J. (2010). *The Microtheory of Innovative Entrepreneurship*. Princeton, NJ: Princeton University Press.

Berman, E. P. (2012). *Creating the Market University*. Princeton, NJ: Princeton University Press.

Blank, S. & B. Dorf (2012). *The Startup Owner's Manual: The Step-By-Step Guide for Building a Great Company*. K & S Ranch.

Bremer, H. W. (2002). "History of Laws and Regulations Affecting the Transfer of Intellectual Property," in T. T. Sherer (Eds.), *AUTM Technology Transfer Practical Manual*, 2nd Edition, Association of University Technology Managers (AUTM).

Brunton, B. (1991). "An Historical Perspective on the Future of the Military-industrial Complex," *The Social Science Journal*, 28(1), 45–62, Elsevier.

Bygrave, W. D. & J. A. Timmons (1995). *Venture Capital at the Crossroads*. Boston, MA: Harvard Business School Press.

Carter, J. (1979). Industrial Innovation Initiatives Message to the Congress on Administration Actions and Proposals. https://www.presidency.ucsb.edu/documents/industrial-innovation-initiatives-message-the-congress-administration-actions-and

Chesbrough, H. (2003). *Open Innovation: The New Imperative for Creating and Profiting from Technology*. Boston, MA: Harvard Business School Press.

Christensen, C. M. (1997). *The Innovator's Dilemma: When New Technologies Cause Great Firms to Fail*. Boston, MA: Harvard Business School Press.

Cohen, I. K., F. Ferretti & B. McIntosh (2014). "Decomposing the Misery Index: A Dynamic Approach," *Cogent Economics & Finance*, 23(1), 1–8.

Cohen, S. S., & Delong, J. B., (2016). *Concrete Economics*, Boston, MA: Harvard Business School Publishing.

DiMaggio, P. J. & W. W. Powell (1983). "The Iron Cage Revisited: Institutional Isomorphism and Collective Rationality in Organizational Fields," *American Sociological Review*, 48, 147–160.

Eisinger, P. K. (1988). *The Rise of the Entrepreneurial State: State and Local Economic Development Policy in the United States*. Madison: University of Wisconsin Press.

Etzkowitz, H. (1996). "Beyond the Frontier: The Convergence of Military and Civilian R&D in the United States," pp. 119–135, in P. Gummertt et al. (eds.), *Military R&D after the Cold War*. Norwell, MA: Kluwer Academic Publisher.

Etzkowitz, H. (2002). *MIT and the Rise of Entrepreneurial Science*. London & New York: Routledge.

Etzkowitz, H. & L. Leydesdorff (2000). "The Dynamics of Innovation: from National Systems and 'Mode 2' to a Triple Helix of University-industry-government Relations," *Research Policy*, 29, 109–123.

Fabrizio, K. R. & D. C. Mowery (2005). "Defense-related R&D and the Growth of the Postwar Information Technology Industrial Complex in the United States," *Revue d'Èconomie Industrielle*, Programme National Persee, 112(1), 27–44.

Feld, B. (2012). *Startup Communities: Building an Entrepreneurial Ecosystem in Your City*. Hoboken, NJ: Wiley & Sons.

Fenn, G. W., J. N. Liang & S. D. Prowse (1995). "The Economics of the Private Equity Market," No. 168, *Staff Studies from Board of Governors of the Federal Reserve System (US)*.

Freeman, C. (1982). *The Economics of Industrial Innovation*, 2nd Edition. Cambridge, MA: MIT Press.

Gibson, D. V. & E. Rogers (1994). *R&D Collaboration on Trial: The Microelectronics and Computer Technology Corporation*. Boston, MA: Harvard Business School Press.

Kneller, R. (1999). "Intellectual Property Rights and University-Industry Technology Transfer in Japan," pp. 307–347, in L. M. Branscomb, F. Kodama, & R. Florida (Eds.), *Industrializing Knowledge*. Cambridge, MA: MIT Press.

Lemann, N. (2019). *Transaction Man: The Rise of the Deal and the Decline of the American Dream*. New York: Farrar, Straus & Giroux.

Leslie, S. W. (1993). *The Cold War and American Science: The Military-Industrial-Academic Complex at MIT and Stanford*. New York: Columbia University Press.

Link, A. N. & J. A. Cunningham (2021). *Advanced Introduction to Technology Policy*. Northampton: Edward Elgar.

Mason, C. M. & R. T. Harrison (1996). "Informal Venture Capital: A Study of the Investment Process, the Post-investment Experience and Investment

Performance," *Entrepreneurship & Regional Development*, 8(2), 105–126. DOI: 10.1080/08985629600000007.

National Academy of Engineering (1980). *Industrial Innovation and Public Policy Options*. Washington, DC: National Academies Press.

National Association of Securities Dealers, Inc. (1987). *The NASDAQ Handbook: The Stock Market of Tomorrow—Today*. Chicago, IL: Probus.

Neal, R. (1999). "Panel I: History and Current Legislative Perspective on the SBIR Program" in C. W. Wessner (Ed.), *The Small Business Innovation Program: Challenges and Opportunities*. Washington, DC: National Academies Press. DOI: 10.17226/9701

Nihon Keizai Shinbun (2021). Morning Edition, June 18.

Nishizawa, A. (2009). "Evolution of Japanese-style Venture Capital and Its Limitation: Why Non-liner VC Model Emerged in Japan," *International Journal of Entrepreneurship and Innovation Management*, 9(4), 416–443.

Nishizawa, A. (2011). "From Triple-Helix Model to Eco-system Building Model," *International Journal of Technoentrepreneurship*, 2(3/4), 304–323.

North, D. C. (1990). *Institutions, Institutional Change and Economic Performance*. Cambridge, UK: Cambridge University Press.

Preer, R. W. (1992). *The Emergence of Technopolis: Knowledge-Intensive Technologies and Regional Development*. New York: Prager.

Servo, J. C. (2005). *Business Planning for Scientists &Engineers*, 4th Edition. Galveston, TX: Dawnbreaker.

Schumpeter, J. A. (2008). *Capitalism, Socialism and Democracy*. New York: Harper-Perennial Modern Thought.

Stein, H. (1994). *Presidential Economics: The Making of Economic Policy from Roosevelt to Clinton,* 3rd Revised Edition. Washington, DC: American Enterprise Institute for Public Policy Research.

Stevens, A. J. (2004). "The Enactment of Bayh-Dole," *Journal of Technology Transfer*, 29, 93–99.

Stokes, D. E. (1997). *Pasteur's Quadrant: Basic Science and Technological Innovation*. Washington, DC: Brookings Institution Press.

Storper, M. (2013). *Keys to the City: How Economics, Institutions, Social Interaction, and Politics Shape Development*. Princeton, NJ: Princeton University Press.

Turner, J. (2006). "The Next Innovation Revolution," *Innovations*, 1(2), 123–144, MIT Press.

VEC (2022). *VEC Year Book 2021* (in Japanese). Venture Enterprise Center Japan.

Wessner, C. W. ed. (1999). *The Small Business Innovation Research Program*. Washington, DC: National Academies Press. DOI: 10.17226/9701

Wessner, C. W. ed. (2008). *An Assessment of the SBIR Program*. Washington, DC: National Academies Press.

Wolff, M. (1980). "The President's Initiatives for Industrial Innovation," *Research Management*, 23(1), 7–12. http://www.jstor.org/stable/24117207

Yoshioka-Kobayashi, T. & M. Takahashi (2022). "Determinants of Contract Renewals in University–industry Contract Research: Going My Way, or Good Sam?" pp. 89–110, in J. M. Azagra-Caro, P. D'Este & D. Barberá-Tomás (Eds.), *University-Industry Knowledge Interactions: People, Tensions and Impact*. Cham: Springer.

2 "New Small i" Institutions of the World's First Technopolis and Key Reasons for Japan's Failed Technopolis Policy

1 Emergence of the World's First Technopolis

As discussed in Chapter 1, strong postwar economic recovery in the United States, Europe, and Japan was underpinned by mass-production industries symbolized by the auto industry, labeled as "Fordist-style" economy. Over time, however, these industrial structures evoked severe economic competition among the United States, Europe, and Japan, and ultimately contributed to severe stagflation of the late 1970s (Boutillier et al., 2016). During this time, Boston—as an innovative outlier—was able to achieve considerable economic growth led by an emerging minicomputer industry evidenced by an agglomeration of related companies located in the circular highway R128, leading to the area being identified as the world's first Technopolis (Botkin, 1988; Preer, 1992, p. 85).

Overcoming a serious economic slump caused by the decline of its leading industries, Boston's academic and business leaders catalyzed and built R&D-based industry on top of its decaying manufacturing economy and in the process became a model for technology-based growth for other US regions and abroad (Preer, 1992, p. 85).[1] Best (2001) identifies underpinning technological change in "Complex System Products" and "Mass Production" that challenged existing industries of New England and Midwest economies from the 1820s to the 1900s; however, these technology advancements also key to growing "Fordist-style" industry that drove the US economy in the 20th century.[2] These technological changes predate Boston's mid-20th century transformation from a declining mature industrial city to a research and development (R&D) digital-based economy that is often referred to as the "Massachusetts Miracle" (Lampe, 1988). Indeed, as discussed below, Boston is a particularly salient and instructive case for other industrialized regions and countries to initiate technology growth policies to reinvent and strengthen declining economies (Preer, 1992).

Preer (1992, p. 11) indicates that, in the late 1970s and early 1980s, Technopolis formation became the "economic holy grail" of development planners and policy makers seeking industrial renaissance with high-tech job creation as they promoted "Technopolis Policies" attempting to emulate

DOI: 10.4324/9781003488149-3

the success of Boston R128.[3] However, as Preer (1992) states, such efforts commonly failed to live up to high expectations because, by design, they replicated the actions that were central to the creation of Boston R128, without taking into account the region's unique geographic, economic, and cultural context. As a result, successful Technopolis development did not occur—even though enthusiastic development planners and policy makers, worldwide, built science parks and business incubators, invested in research, established venture capital funds, and formed all manner of public-private partnerships. Preer (1992) notes that a lack of "Technopolis Policy economic theory" inhibited such development in contrast to how "Keynesian economics" was important to enhancing economic development after World War II.

Preer (1992) described a "Framework for Technopolis Policy Analysis" by defining Technopolis as "a region that generates sustained and economic activity through the creation and commercialization of new knowledge" (Preer, 1992, p. 55). He observed the existence of strategies and structures in Boston R128 (i.e., science parks and business incubators) as perhaps being important. Yet these entities were not sufficient for growing a tech-based economy (Preer, 1992). Preer's analysis defined Technopolis formation—not from a static perspective of clustering research entities, science parks, and high-tech firms—but from a dynamic perspective of creative processes to develop new knowledge which could then be translated into high-tech products and services. Based on this dynamic perspective, his "Technopolis Policy Analysis Framework" clarified the necessary conditions for the formation of a Technopolis as being composed of (1) "Knowledge Centers" to develop new science and technology, and (2) "Innovative Environments" to transform emerging new knowledge into commercialized products and services.

In short with the "Technopolis Policy Analysis Framework," Preer (1992) identified "Knowledge Centers" and "Innovative Environments" as necessary conditions for the emergence of Boston R128 as a Technopolis; however, he did not propose concrete measures or models on how to build "Innovative Environments." While he suggested that "Innovative Environments" should be composed of specific factors such as a pool of skilled labor, knowledge infrastructure, and significant information resources embodied in people and entities, he did not offer viable measures or models for the nurturing processes needed to enable such specific factors (Preer, 1992).

2 Building "New Small i" Institutions

Storper (2013, p. 227) states that "Small i" institutions are critical to regional economic growth and an important component of any theoretical perspective concerning Technopolis development. He emphasizes that existing urban growth theories did not clarify the causes of "Winners and Losers" in the economic development of modern US cities.[4] He supports the idea that New Economic Geography (NEG), presented as the Dixit-Stiglitz-Krugman (DSK) Model, could help identify the sequenced processes of urban economic change from growth and maturity to decline, but he also contends that NEG cannot explain the phenomenon of modern cities regarding the widening of the gap between "Winners and Losers" and the rebirth of declining economically mature cities like Boston. Storper (2013, p. 93) argues that the economic development of modern cities lies in "knowledge rent" brought by "the invention of a key market-changing technology" as the seed of disruptive innovation. He also notes that, for "knowledge rent" to contribute to long-term urban economic growth, it is essential to transform "knowledge rent" into "Romer externalities" which bring increasing returns by diffusion into the urban economy.[5] Romer (1992) stipulates that knowledge, as a non-rival good, cannot maintain its "excludability" without a system of specialized intellectual property rights protection. In response to Romer's stipulation, Storper notes that while a patent exploitation system is a necessary "New Capital I" institution for bringing about "Romer externalities," it is not a sufficient condition to sustain long-term urban economic growth unless the patent exploitation system is built as a national-level "Capital I" institution (Storper, 2013, pp. 52–66).

Storper (2013) presents biotech clusters as an example of how converting and maintaining "knowledge rent" into "Romer externalities" has led to long-term urban economic growth in cities like San Francisco, San Diego, and Boston,[6] where "knowledge rent" was maintained as "Romer externalities" by specific local conditions. Storper (2013) stresses the importance of "the diversity of organizational forms, the presence of 'anchor tenants' (i.e., successful growth firms) operating under norms of openness, and cross-domain network connections as these factors help maintain "Romer externalities" (Storper, 2013, p. 129).

Storper further emphasizes "actor-networks" as important in fulfilling specific local conditions which enable the diffusion and maintenance of "Romer externalities" in a particular city sustaining long-term economic growth. After stipulating that Silicon Valley represents the development of a modern urban economy based on "knowledge rent" brought by "the invention of key market-changing technology," Storper also insists that it was "robust actors," such as William Shockley, Gordon Moore, Fred Terman, Stewart Brand, Alf Heller, Steve Jobs, the people at Xerox Parc, and many others, whose actions-built Silicon Valley's institutions. He identifies the importance of "the actor-networks of the merchant semi-conductor producers and their culture of open competition to capture the industry, and that this generated the specialization the region still enjoys today in having the highest per capita income in the world's wealthiest economy" (Storper, 2013, pp. 136–137).

Importantly, Storper concludes that the Bay Area's "antiestablishment counterculture" was an essential condition for the acceptance and success of these robust actors and their actor-networks as core Silicon Valley's institutions (Storper, 2013, pp. 134–138). In short, he regards local culture as a critically important variable to building Silicon Valley's institutions and enabling tech-based economic growth through actor-networks built by "robust actors." While regional culture and actor networks are seen as key to technology development in both Boston and Silicon Valley, Storper (2013) and Preer (1992) also stress the importance of Department of Defense's (DOD) military R&D policies for jump-starting post-World War R&D that became the foundation of the US national system of innovation. These initiatives were largely enacted from 1945 to 1950, when peaceful demobilization was replaced by Cold War rearmament (Storper, 2013, p. 189). Indeed, as Preer (1992, p. 100) notes, "defense spending was an important market for high-technology businesses in Boston R128 and Silicon Valley," and these regions were catalyzed by DOD's military R&D policies. It is important to understand that these policies impacted only a limited area of DOD's military R&D as it did not include private sector R&D. In keeping with our current research, an important question is why DOD's military R&D policies stimulated a system of innovation in Boston R128 and Silicon Valley, but these same policies did not catalyze regional technology development in other US regions with well-respected research universities.

3   Boston R128 and "Robust Actors"

Innovative DOD military R&D policies were formulated in response to a technology paradigm shift to computer-based digital technology during the "Globalization of the Cold War" that precipitated new government-industry-academia collaborations called "the military-industrial-academic complex" (Leslie, 1993, p. 2). While Leslie (1993, p. 12) agrees that Boston R128 and Silicon Valley were the by-products of massive military spending under the DOD's new military R&D policies, he does not explain why such outcomes were limited to these two regions. Indeed, "the military-industrial-academic complex" initially benefitted MIT, followed by Stanford University, while other prominent US research universities tended to avoid military-related technological R&D to preserve the "independence of the ivory tower" university model following World War II (Leslie, 1993; Geiger, 2004). Etzkowitz (1996, p. 127) notes that at the time MIT and Stanford were "anomalies within the US academic system." Indeed, in Boston, despite the decline of textile and related machinery industries, there remained a strong advocacy for continued support of these industries—as well as opposition to nurturing high-tech companies launched by the commercialization of MIT's research results (Etzkowitz, 2002).

Preer (1992) identifies Ralph Flanders (President of the Federal Reserve Bank of Boston), Karl Compton (MIT President), George Doriot (Professor of Industrial Management at the Harvard Business School), and Kenneth Olsen (the founder of Digital Equipment Corporation (DEC)) as especially important "robust actors" in Boston's economic transformation. Importantly, these "robust actors" reformed policy proposals for "Existing Capital I" institutions and built vital "New Capital I" and "New Small i" institutions. For example, Flanders and Compton established the New England Council, involving the local business community to change Boston's economic policy.

Thus, they gained regional support to move from a focus of saving existing companies in outdated industries to building "New Small i" institutions that might help tech-based startups to commercialize market-changing technologies emerging from MIT. Together, Flanders and Compton enabled MIT to become the entrepreneurial university which they saw as an essential component to implementing needed new policies (Etzkowitz, 2002).

Foss and Gibson (2015, p. 1) define the entrepreneurial university as one that embraces "the third mission of 'service' with a concerted effort to help stimulate and sustain economic development" in addition to the university's traditional first and second academic missions of education and research. To implement the third mission, an entrepreneurial university needs to facilitate "use-inspired basic research" in the fields of physics and mathematics resulting in inventions of key market-changing technologies, such as semiconductor and computer technologies and the practical application of digital technologies (Rosenbloom & Spencer, 1996). The advancement of digital technology increased the need for "Use-inspired Basic Research" and the shift from industry-university separation to industry-university collaboration. As a result, increasing numbers of research universities have undergone institutional change to become more entrepreneurial including implementing such structures as University-Industry Research Centers (UIR), Office of Technology Licensing (OTL), Research Parks, and other related facilities (Etzkowitz, 2002; Berman, 2012). Table 2.1 provides an overview of important characteristics of an entrepreneurial university.

A for-profit research culture—important for the commercialization of new knowledge obtained through "Use-inspired Basic Research"—is often seen to be in conflict with the "Open, Share, Non-profit" culture of "Pure Basic Research." There is ample criticism within and outside many research universities that such reforms would negatively impact established academic missions that focus on knowledge creation apart from profit-seeking. Indeed, MIT's President Compton, together with Vice President Vannevar Bush, thought it best to reconcile the third mission within the university's existing education and research activities by establishing an off-campus military-industry collaborative R&D center called the Radiation Laboratory (Rad Lab). The Rad Lab assisted in dealing with conflicting interests on research activities by establishing a 20% rule for consulting university researchers, 50% overhead from external research funds, formalized contracts for industry-academia-government collaboration, and establishing MIT's ownership of patents and policies. Importantly, the Research Corporation of New York established a Boston office becoming MIT's OTL (Eztkowitz, 2002). These innovative strategies and institutional changes contributed to MIT being awarded significant DOD funding for research focused on digital technologies. Additionally, the allocation of overhead to revitalizing academic missions and other educational activities contributed to MIT becoming and sustaining itself as an internationally recognized top ranked research and teaching university (Etzkowitz, 2002).[7]

Table 2.1 Characteristics of a University's Entrepreneurial Architecture

Entrepreneurial Architecture	Description (according to Nelles & Vorley, 2010)	Examples and Link to Third Mission
Structures	Formal organizational mechanism of knowledge exchange such as offices or departments within the university.	Technology Transfer Offices (TTOs) official positions, offices. Classes focused on formal third mission activities, learning labs with live data/problem sets. Institutionalizing societal engagements. Establishment of centers of excellence, etc.
Systems	Networks of communication and coordination. Norms of interaction. Embedded values.	Decentralized TTO systems (narrow view). Informal third mission activities. Initiating societal engagements.
Strategies	Third mission/ stream organizational goals and avenues	Strategy documents contain third mission goals.
Leadership	Key leadership roles and their influence on strategic decisions	Leadership conceives and spearheads third mission activities.
Culture	Attitudes of individuals and the value they place on innovation and entrepreneurial activities.	To what degree third mission activities are admired and respected/understood as such.

Source: Oftedal et al. (2022). Further referencing Nelles and Vorley (2010).

A similar transformation at Stanford University was led by Dean of Engineering, Frederick Terman, whose thesis advisor at MIT was Vannevar Bush. Terman came to Stanford University as an assistant professor of engineering in 1925, becoming the dean of the School of Engineering in 1951 and provost from 1955 to 1965. During his tenure at Stanford, Terman focused on expanding the science, statistics, and engineering departments to help win more research grants from the DOD. He also spearheaded the creation of Stanford Industrial Park (now Stanford Research Park) as an innovative model where the university leased portions of land to high-tech firms—one of the first being Hewlett-Packard, whose founders were Terman's students Bill Hewlett and David Packard. Research grants, in addition to funds that patented research generated, helped catapult Stanford to become a first-class educational and research institution in consort with spurring the tech-based growth of Silicon Valley. Terman's efforts to create a mutual relationship between Stanford and the regionally based tech companies significantly contributed to this growth. Speaking of this effort, Terman remembered, "When we set out to create a community of technical scholars in Silicon Valley, there wasn't much here and the rest of the world looked awfully big. Now a lot of the rest of the world is here" (Wikipedia, Palo Alto History Project 2010-01-16 at the Wayback Machine).

The mutual relationship between Stanford and regionally based tech companies and government programs is well exemplified by NASA's Ames Research Center, which is at the heart of Silicon Valley, both geographically and figuratively (Terdiman, 2007). NASA's Apollo program relied heavily on researchers from Stanford, nearby University of California at Berkeley, and a number of small regional companies beginning in the 1960s and government contracts played a key role. The Apollo program was an important source of technology that would eventually lead to commercial products and applications. Among the companies that benefitted most was Hewlett-Packard. The Apollo program also allowed early semiconductor companies like Intel to develop a transformative technology at government expense, a technology that would have broad application and whose price would plummet as these companies perfected manufacturing methods.

At MIT, while the transition to an entrepreneurial university was a crucial component of the creation of Boston as a Technopolis, important additional support institutions were needed to launch and grow startup companies that would commercialize MIT's research results. For example, the "New Products Committee," organized in 1939 by the New England Council, cited Boston's lack of funding for startups as an important weakness. George Doriot, a member of this committee, recommended the creation of new funding organizations, and he also emphasized tech-based startups required a "new kind of manager."

In response to Doriot's recommendations, Ralph Flanders proposed an innovative investment vehicle dedicated to supporting tech-based startups. He observed that Boston's low rate of new industry creation was not due to a lack of capital, but due to a lack of capital dedicated to investing in regional startups (Jacobs, 1969, p. 193). Boston, as a mature industrialized city, had a notable defect in that it did not financially support regional tech-based startups to launch, grow, and agglomerate, even while breakthrough technologies emerged from use-inspired research activities at MIT (Nicholas, 2019). The American Research Development Corporation (ARD), the world's first venture capital (VC), was launched by Flanders in 1946 with the assistance of Compton and Doriot (Preer, 1992). Doriot followed Flanders as ARD's second president and established ARD as a VC company with a business model that would differentiate itself from existing private capital entities by adopting a systematic investment approach of institutional investors (Nicholas, 2019). Importantly, he set ARD's investment targets based on the combination of funding excellent talent and innovative technology—and ARD's staff often became directors of portfolio companies and supported them during their assessment by the ARD Technical Advisory Board (Figure 2.1).

As a result of its early investment in DEC, ARD became quite successful and presented a national model illustrating the high potential for VC investment. Interestingly, Nicholas (2019) notes that the most important aspect of

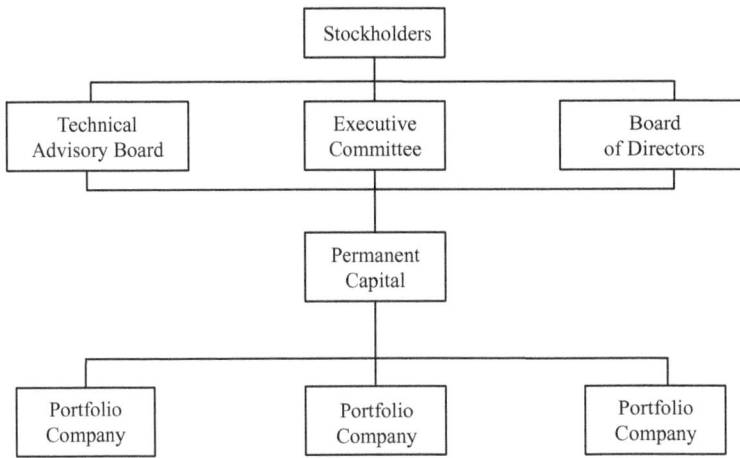

Figure 2.1 The Organizational Structure of ARD

Source: Nicholas (2019, p. 118)

ARD's success was the "middling returns ARD generated from its portfolio firms, which were viewed as risky and failing" (p. 130). Interestingly, Doriot established ARD's business model as one that emphasized company and job creation over investment returns (Gupta, 2004).[8] Another distinctive feature of ARD was the management support it provided to portfolio companies through mentors and the Technology Advisory Board. Indeed, Kenneth Olson, founder of DEC, credits ARD with playing an important role of mentor and champion. Bygrave and Timmons (1992) contend that General Doriot's creation of ARD was, in itself, a great entrepreneurial activity. They also note that "ARD was what Schumpeter had in mind when he wrote about new types of organization that transform economies" (p. 122). Storper (2013, p. 129) stresses the importance of anchor tenants (i.e., initial successful firms) "operating under norms of openness, and cross-domain network connections" to transpose "Small i" institutions. In the case of Boston R128, DEC (as the main anchor tenant) stimulated the development of "New Small i" institutions while commercializing cutting-edge technologies that emerged out of DOD's new military R&D policies.

Importantly, at the time of DEC's founding, Olsen drew up a business plan that did not depend on the military as its sole or main customer—in contrast to tech-based startups from Lincoln Lab that heavily depended on the military. IBM's 7090 mainframe computer was largely marginalized as MIT students lined up to use DEC's Personal Data Processor (PDP) "Whirlwind," an offspring that enabled real-time computing and "was by all computing standards a radical product" (Rifkin, 1990, p. 40; Gupta, 2004, p. 62). DEC's first minicomputer, PDP-1, was inferior in computing power compared to IBM and Universal Automatic Computer (UNIVAC) mainframe computers; however, it delivered high performance and met user expectations with smaller size at a lower price. Most importantly, PDP-1 allowed for interactive computing and visualizing data-handling through a Cathode Ray Tube (CRT) display.

In 1962, five years after launching DEC, ITT Inc. (International Telephone and Telegraph) entered a major purchase contract for PDP-1 due to its superiority as a telephone switching system controller—validating DEC's minicomputer manufacturer business (Rifkin & Harrar, 1990) as well as realizing ARD's investment strategy focused on early positive results. After this success, "DEC combined low price with impressive functionality and high-end performance. In 1960, the PDP-1 sold for $120,000 ($1 million today), but by 1965, the PDP-8 dropped to a $18,000 price point ($140,000 today), making it the first mass-produced minicomputer" (Nicholas, 2019, p. 129). "The PDP-8 defined an industry and sent DEC sales into orbit and the company grew between 25 and 40 percent per year in revenue as well as profit for the next seventeen years" (Rifkin & Harrar, 1990, p. 70). According to Nicholas (2019), this rapid growth led to DEC's Initial Public Offering (IPO) in 1966 and by the end of 1971, DEC was worth an extraordinary $355 million to ARD in unrealized gains. Beyond that, this success confirmed the vision of ARD's founders that investing in innovative firms could accelerate regional growth, build wealth, and attract talent. Nicholas (2019 p. 129) also clarified that in the early 1970s DEC became the largest employer in Massachusetts, and America's second largest computer manufacturer next to IBM.

DEC's success as an "anchor tenant" inspired other Boston area engineers and scientists to develop new products and enterprises (Dorfman, 1988, p. 257). Dorfman notes, "it appears that in the postwar era, new firms were in a better position to find venture capital in Boston than in many other parts of the country" (p. 255). Additionally, the growth of tech-based startups led to increased numbers of professional service providers (i.e., legal, accounting, and business consulting) who focused on accelerating the growth of regional minicomputer-related companies. These regional agglomeration advantages enhanced hardware and software developments for the minicomputer as Boston R128 grew its technological and services base.

The burgeoning minicomputer industry rejuvenated Boston's economy and became known as "Massachusetts Miracle" (Dorfman, 1988). Boston R128 was formed by "Romer externality" maintaining "knowledge rent" through the innovative contributions of ARD and DEC, which commercialized key market-changing technologies that emerged from MIT under the DOD's military R&D policies. Robust actions taken by Flanders, Compton, Doriot, and Olsen fulfilled the necessary and sufficient conditions indispensable for transposing "Existing Small i" to "New Small i" institutions in Boston and thereby helped transform MIT through organizations such as ARD, which proved pivotal in the growth of tech-based startups in the emerging minicomputer industry. A regional culture of supporting innovation and entrepreneurship was born through the agglomeration of minicomputer-related tech-based startups (Dorfman, 1988, p. 257)—and (we posit) the transition of "Existing Small i" to "New Small i" institutions by "robust actors."

4 Japan's Failed Technopolis Building Efforts

After postwar reconstruction, the Japanese manufacturing economy had emerged as a strong competitor to European and US companies especially in the export-oriented "Fordist-style industries" such as mass-production electric appliances and automobiles. This was the result of "Existing Capital I" institutions, in which the Japanese central government, especially the Ministry of International Trade and Industry (MITI) selected target industries to be promoted, as they provided fiscal and financial incentives to realize their policies through the creation of products that combined low price and high quality through incremental innovation in target industries. Japan achieved successful economic competition with the United States through high-quality production while reducing costs through a high-operating ratio of manufacturing facilities that resulted in an export offensive to escape stagflation. However, Japan was unable to depend on its marginalized domestic market which was limited by income disparities and a dual structure of big businesses and small and medium-sized enterprises (SMEs).

In our view, to escape from stagflation, Japan needed to transition from "Existing Capital I" to "New Capital I" institutions in consort with the creation of "New Small i" institutions targeting R&D-based domestic industry and market growth. Silicon Valley's rapid growth in the late 1970s attracted considerable attention in Japan, and it became an imperative policy mission to duplicate such success. Many Japanese researchers, policy makers, and corporate executives visited Northern California as they attempted to understand the secrets of Silicon Valley's vibrant economic growth. However, after many visits and observations, Japanese policy makers and private business leaders recognized the difficulty of successfully duplicating Silicon Valley-type tech-based economic growth due to considerable cultural and social differences. Also, there were no clear viable models to be followed for such a strategy. But, one observation, which seemed integral, was the close academia-industry-government R&D collaboration that existed at Stanford University.

In the 1970s, there were two major R&D centers in Japan: Tsukuba Science City and Tokyo. It was believed by Japanese policy makers that Tsukuba could not foster the necessary innovations for tech-based economic growth because, as they saw it, the universities and national laboratories focused on discovery-oriented basic research without collaborating with each other or with the private sector. Yet, in Tokyo, electronics companies were dominated by cultures of imitation and excessive domestic competition. Accordingly, policy makers realized there was a need to foster innovation that was different from existing Japanese-style R&D institutions, and it needed to be based on new strong cooperation among academic, industry, and government sectors (Tatsuno, 1986).

Toshiyuki Chikami, the Mayor of Kurume City, in Kyushu—having worked at Japan's MITI—named his city "Technopolis" to signify the transformation from a sluggish local city to a vibrant tech-hub city with financial assistance from the central government. The idea and name of "Technopolis" coined by Chikami was immediately adopted by Japan's special committee investigating MITI's new industrial policy, and "Technopolis Policy" became quite popular by suggesting a viable path to rejuvenate Japan's regional economies as stated in *The Industrial Policy Vision in 1980s* published by MITI (MITI, 1980; Tatsuno, 1986). Japan's Technopolis Policy attracted wide attention among government and policy makers as an effective rejuvenation plan for regional economies suffering from stagflation. Through the power of locally elected Diet members, regional governments put strong pressure on Japan's central government to implement Technopolis Policy as a regional economic recovery policy to transform the nation's export-oriented Fordist-style industries. While existing institutions had indeed brought successful postwar reconstruction and high economic growth to Japan, the high-tech industries exemplified by Silicon Valley were seen as a way to move the Japanese economy beyond stagflation and accelerate regional economic growth (Tatsuno, 1986).

We contend that Japan's Technopolis Policy might be better characterized as a "playing catchup" policy to proliferate newly developed integrated circuit (IC) technologies following the United States, rather than to meaningfully transpose Japan's "Existing Capital I" institutions. Compared to the United States, Japan's IC production capacity in the early 1970s was extremely low, and the new Technopolis Policy supported opening new plants to expand IC mass production with the state-of-the-art equipment, obtained through Japan's "Very Large-Scale Integration (VLSI) Project." As of 1976, this government-industry R&D consortium aimed to fill the technology gap and build a technological foundation for Japan's electronics industry (Gibson & Rogers, 1994; Tarui, 2000).[9] Through infrastructure subsidiaries, financial support, and tax incentives, Japan's Technopolis Policy supported big businesses to establish large-scale IC production plants.[10] As a result of IC factory stimulus, such plants were built in Kyushu in the south and Tohoku in the north, which were called Silicon Island and Silicon Road, respectively. Strong MITI initiatives subsidized hard infrastructure construction with financial support and tax incentives (Tatsuno, 1986).[11] Initially, these two regions were recognized as successful cases of Japan's Technopolis Policy to establish and expand IC manufacturing factories.[12] Yet these results proved ephemeral as trade imbalances caused the Yen to soar.

The Plaza Accord of 1985 caused a sharp appreciation of the yen and a crisis in existing industries that resulted in strong pressure for major manufacturing facilities to relocate to lower cost Asian countries, including the newly constructed IC manufacturing factories, abandoning newly designated Japanese Technopolis regions. Deindustrialization became a major concern and Japan's Technopolis Policy was forced to change its target from inducing big IC chip manufacturing facilities to regionally based endogenous high-tech industry formation that required a strong transposition to "New Capital I" institutions.

One symbolic event that was evoked by this change began in 1987 with the establishment of Regional Joint Research Centers (RJRCs) at national universities[13] in support of the promise of innovative academia-industry-government collaboration (Table 2.2). However, the establishment of RJRCs spread, not only to Japan's national universities in the Technopolis-designated areas but to many other national universities. From 1987 to 1998, 3–5 new RJRCs were established each year, and by 1998, 52 RJRCs had been established among the 99 national universities, with 20 of these located in Technopolis-designated areas (Table 2.2). Most of these efforts were initiated by the prefectural governments rather than national universities that were in each prefecture. Indeed, national universities responded rather passively to prefectural government requests to enhance their budgets as there was deep-rooted opposition to industry-academia collaboration especially at Japan's top research universities (Suzuki, 2001).

With its stove-piped central governmental administration, the Ministry of Education was hesitant for national universities to become involved in industrial policy,[14] which was traditionally under the jurisdiction of MITI. So, while it is undeniable that Technopolis Policy's target change became the important trigger to give Japan's national universities a new mission, the RJRCs were unable to perform the same function as the US-type UIRCs (Tatsuno, 1986). Unfortunately, no "robust actors" emerged in Japan to lead the transformation from ivory tower research university to entrepreneurial university as was the case with Compton at MIT and Terman at Stanford. Furthermore, while Japanese VCs were able to acquire critical financing for their growth in the early 1980s, they were unable to fulfill the VC model that Doriot had realized in Boston 128. Beginning in 1982, Japanese VCs had expanded their investment in tech-based startups through American-style partnership VC funds.[15]

However, as many tech-based startups went bankrupt after 1985 due to the soaring Yen, Japanese VCs sought alternative investment opportunities to improve their investment performance. In the late 1980s, Japan was at the height of a bubble economy featuring the service sectors' growing medium-sized companies emerging as anchor-tenants, while improving the quality of life within an affluent society brought by a bubble economy. Japan's VCs achieved relatively high investment performance through these service sector companies which were able to achieve IPOs. To weather the economic crisis when the yen soared in 1985, Japan's VCs drastically changed their investment focus, transforming themselves into "principal investing firms" while continuing to call themselves VC firms.[16] They functioned in response to structural changes in bank-centered corporate finance, which was part of the "Existing Capital I" institution system, rather than in deconstructing mature companies. Even by the late 1980s, Japan had not yet

Table 2.2 Establishment of RJRCs at Japanese National Universities

FY	National Universities	Universities with RJRCs	In Technopolis Area	Names of National University
1987	95	3	2	Toyama[x], Kobe, Kumamoto[x]
1988	95	5	0	Muroran Tech., Gunma, Tokyo A&M, Gifu, Nagoya[*]
1989	96	5	1	Ibaragi, Utsunomiya[x], Nagoya Tech., Kyushu Tech, Saga
1990	96	5	3	Yamanashi[x], Mie, Kyoto T&T, Okayama[x], Nagasaki[x]
1991	96	5	2	Yokohama, Niigata, Shizuoka[x], Yamaguchi[x], Tokushima
1992	96	5	2	Kitami Tech., Yamagata[x], Tokyo E&C, Fukui, Kagoshima[x]
1993	96	5	4	Iwate[x], Akita[x], Shinshu[x], Tottori, Oita[x]
1994	96	5	2	Saitama, Chiba, Ehime[x], Kyushu[*], Miyazaki[x]
1995	98	5	1	Kanazawa, Osaka[*], Hiroshima[x], Kochi, Ryukyu
1996	98	4	1	Hokkaido[xx], Obihiro A&VM, Tokyo[*], Shimane
1997	99	2	1	Hirosaki[x], Kyushu T&D
1998	99	3	1	Tohoku[xx], Tokyo Tech., Kobe M.
Total	99	52	20	

Note: [x]shows Technopolis Core University and [*] shows former Imperial Universities.

Source: Reprinted from p. 96 of Suzuki (2001).

broken away from "Existing Capital I" institutional forms that supported postwar reconstruction (Nishizawa, 2009).[17] From the mid-1980s,[18] Japan's growing bubble economy spawned overconfidence in its existing industries, its economic structures, and performance projections without deeply exploring necessary structural change from Fordist-style analogue technology to knowledge-based digital technology. During the bubble economy, even regions with stagnant economies, due to relocating manufacturing plants to Association of Southeast Asian Nations (ASEAN), tended to expect a trickledown of economic wealth without pursuing endogenous tech-based economic growth as envisioned by Japan's Technopolis Policy (Ito, 1998).

In summary, Japan's Technopolis Policy failed to build effective "New Capital I" institutions and "New Small i" institutions as occurred in Boston R128 and Silicon Valley. Japanese researchers, policy makers, and business leaders mistakenly believed that successful Technopolis could be formed by macro or regulative policies alone. They did not fully appreciate the importance of necessary change in a range of sectors including (1) the relationship between "New Capital I" and "New Small i" institutions, (2) the need to evolve toward entrepreneurial universities, (3) the role of academia-industry-government collaborative R&D in tech-based startups, (4) the building processes of "New Small i" institutions, and (5) the importance of "robust actors" in motivating underlying conditions needed for Technopolis development as was the case in Boston R128 and Silicon Valley.[19] Importantly, the theoretical understanding for the importance of these changes did not exist in the early 1980s as there were no academic studies that had fully investigated the theoretical requirements for the necessity of building "New Capital I" and "New Small i" institutions and the important roles of "robust actors." Accordingly, after the bubble economy burst, there remained the challenge to transpose "Existing Capital I" to "New Capital I" institutions supplemented by the creation of regionally based "New Small i" institutions.

Notes

1 While it is common for Silicon Valley to be seen and studied as the primary US Technopolis model, we suggest that Boston R128 provides exceptional clarifications from regional policy and institutional development perspectives. The Boston case provides important insights on how to rejuvenate a regional economy with a declining industry base which is perhaps a more common situation than the "green fields" model of Silicon Valley.

2 Brezis and Krugman (1997) presented a growth-theoretic model in which technological change between old and new leads to a transposition from old to new cities. If we summarize this model using learning effect, capital rent, and transaction cost, it can be concluded that, in the cities developed with existing technology (old cities), the capital rent obtained by adopting new technology is low compared to existing technology due to the poor learning effect of new technology. In contrast, the new city being unrelated to existing technologies can obtain capital rent from the adoption of new technologies due to lower transaction costs, such as land and transportation costs. The case of Boston R128 is an example of an older city growing through the adoption of new technology.

3 The "Technopolis" label was coined by Japan's "Technopolis Policy" in the early 1980s (Preer, 1992) and over time became a popular label and regional economic development objective in identifiable locations in the United States, Europe, and Asia (Smilor et al., 1988; Gibson et al., 1992; Castells & Hall, 1994). "Technopolis" has been defined as the modern city-state linking technology and economic development precipitated by (1) a major technological paradigm shift, (2) increased globalization, and (3) organizational change of production and management styles (Smilor et al., 1988, p. xvii; Castells & Hall, 1994, pp. 2–4). These three transformative changes are categorized as a driving force for both industrialized and newly industrializing countries in the pursuit of strategies to duplicate the technology growth success of Silicon Valley and Route 128 (Preer, 1992, p. 2; Castells & Hall, 1994, pp. 2–3).

4 Storper (2013) defined the top ten US cities and the bottom five US cities as "Winners and Losers" in terms of income decline between 1980 and 2000 based on the population and nominal income growth rate as he identified the cause of these differentials within the same country.

5 Storper (2013) states that long-term urban economic growth is brought by disruptive innovation, but that the equilibrium theory of neoclassical economics cannot clarify this long-term urban growth and that it is necessary to rely on the Romer growth model, which focuses on endogenous economic growth. In the Romer growth model, Marshall's externality is defined as the increasing returns

of knowledge rent evoked by innovation as the source of long-term urban economic growth. This perspective also emphasizes the importance of intellectual property systems including patent laws that can give knowledge, as a non-rival good excludability, as rent (Warsh, 2006).

6 Powell et al. (2012) note that, in 1982, there were at least 20 universities in the United States with top research achievements in biological science and only three cities with biomedical patent filings. Powell called this phenomenon "the Puzzle of Space." The importance of "Entrepreneurial Ecosystem," place-based research, has increased since 2013, but it has not yet provided a sufficient solution to "the Puzzle of Space" due to the polysemy of "Ecosystem" introduced as biological analogy and the proliferation of issues such as its conceptual definition, functions, and outcomes (Cavallo et al., 2019, "Entrepreneurial Ecosystem Research: Present Debates and Future Directions," *International Entrepreneurship and Management Journal*, 15(4), pp. 1–24).

7 As a background of MIT's transformation as an entrepreneurial university before other research universities, Etzkowitz clarified that "MIT integrated various academic formats, including the classical teaching college, the polytechnic engineering school, the land grant university and the research university into a unique configuration" (Etzkowitz, 2002, p. 20). President Compton's reforms institutionalized innovative academic formats, including the classical teaching college, the polytechnic engineering school, the land grant university, and the research university. Etzkowitz (1996, p. 127) noted that these innovative administrative actions in the early 1980s precipitated a "second academic revolution" where MIT and Stanford, which had been anomalies within the US academic system, became models for other universities to emulate.

8 ARD proved the effectiveness of "long tail" investments that follow the "power law" through successful DEC investments. While "ARD is widely recognized as a key entity in the evolution of the modern venture capital industry" (Nicholas, 2019, p. 109; Mallaby, 2022), it was strictly regulated under 1940 Investment Company Act and Tax Exemption Regulation because of the failure to introduce the Limited Partnership Model (LPM) that did not adopt the VC's important funding scheme. Kenny (2001) insisted that LPM is "the single most important organizational innovation of the modern venture capital system" which became popular in the early 1960s because of their extremely suitable structure for VC investment with inviting successful entrepreneurs as limited partners.

9 The IC industry in Japan lagged in manufacturing compared to Europe and the United States until the mid-1970s. Planning to overcome this gap, MITI established the VLSI Project in 1976. MITI (in cooperation with other government ministries) formed public-private collaborative R&D consortia, inviting big businesses such as Fujitsu, Hitachi, NEC, Mitsubishi Electric, and TOSHIBA to work together to develop targeted technologies. Highly productive Japanese IC manufacturing devices emerged in the early 1980s from the VLSI project and huge national investments in IC chip manufacturing facilities. IC chips were expected to be used in word processors, related office machines, game consoles, and electric home appliances. While IC chip manufacturing facilities required large-scale plants and equipment with high electricity and water usage, the resulting IC chip was light, thin, and small, and had low transportation costs compared to the products of smokestack heavy industries. IC chip manufacturing factories did not have the same location requirements as heavy and chemical industries which had brought high-economic growth and postwar reconstruction to Japan. Furthermore, IC chip manufacturing created high-tech jobs that required a more highly educated workforce and the domestic retention high-tech talent (Tarui, 2000).

10 The Technopolis Law provided (1) private for-profit company investments in a "Technopolis Developing Agency" were allowed as pecuniary loss under the tax

law; (2) increased local allocation taxes, which compensated local governments for the decreasing fixed assets taxes due to the law's deduction of R&D assets in Technopolis areas; (3) deregulation for local government bond projects that provided infrastructure in a Technopolis area; and (4) eased the Farmland Law to facilitate transferring farmlands to industrial zones. In addition to these policies, the Technopolis Law carried out budgetary measures, tax preferences, and low-rate lending; established Techno-mart to facilitate IP exchange and Research-core as the R&D center in the Technopolis areas; and required relocation of private company R&D under the Key Facilities Siting Law. Importantly, the Technopolis Law provided tax preference—including accelerated depreciation for high-tech R&D facilities, factories, and related buildings valued at more than 1 billion yen, as well as tax exemption for owning land valued at more than 100 million yen— providing high incentives for locating IC manufacturing facilities to a designated Technopolis areas.

11 Preer pointed out that while Technopolis Policy normally emphasized the development of "invisible" infrastructure to meet a knowledge-based "new industrial era," Japan's Technopolis Policy emphasized visible infrastructure; for example, access to the bullet train's stations and expressways was legislated as an important unique feature (Preer, 1992).

12 The major Japanese electronics manufacturers that participated in the VSLI project were able to use IC chips supplied by the large-scale production plants supported by the Technopolis policy not only for newly developed electrical products such as personal computers and CD players but also for improving the performance of existing electrical products such as electric rice cookers and washing machines. These benefits enabled them to realize economies of scale and strengthened their competitiveness through lower prices for IC chips. Florida and Kenney (1990) found that while Japanese electrical manufacturers excelled in the incremental innovations possible in follow-through applications of advanced technologies such as IC chips, Silicon Valley high-tech startups, which were biased toward disruptive innovation, failed to apply such breakthrough technologies to existing industries. In retrospect, however, it seems that Japan's industry-government-academia joint R&D organizations often relied on large corporations that were unable to create disruptive innovations. This can be pointed out as an institutional flaw of Japanese-style R&D that led to the prolonged stagnation after the bubble burst. In fact, following the success of the VSLI project, although MITI established the Institute for New Generation Computer Technology (ICOT) to develop hardware and software for a new generation of computers that would surpass IBM's mainframes, ICOT failed to develop any disruptive innovations and was eventually closed. Furthermore, the industry-academia-government R&D organization for the development of high-definition television in Japan, led by public broadcaster NHK for more than 25 years, supported by MITI and the Postal Service, involving major consumer electronics manufacturers, was defeated by Video Cypher (acquired as a division of General Instrument Corporation) which succeeded in creating disruptive innovation called digital hi-vision (Brinkley, 1997). Since then, Japan's major consumer electronics manufacturers have fallen behind the low-cost offensive of Asian manufacturers (especially in mainland China) in creating disruptive innovations through the commercialization of digital technology. The major Japanese consumer electronics manufacturers that once "shook the United States" went into decline, only to be bailed out by Chinese and Taiwanese companies.

13 After the end of World War II in 1949, in hopes of providing equal opportunities in higher education, Japan founded a new university system with "one national university per prefecture," modeled after the state universities of the United States. However, most national universities continued to ignore involvement in

the local economy, prioritizing research on the "ivory tower" model. While the establishment of RJRCs in 1987 could be appreciated as a historical trigger in Japanese national university institutions, in reality, the research system of RJRCs initiated by prefectural governments was not effective. It was not until the end of the 1990s, when Japan's Technopolis Policy ended, that academia-industry-government collaboration began to take off. In the 1990s, the "daigakuin jutenka (expanding and diversification of graduate school education and research)" programs were introduced by the Ministry of Education to incorporate the research university concept, but the Ministry of Education did not recognize entrepreneurial universities at that time. Under the National University Corporation Act of 2003, national universities were incorporated and allowed to own and utilize intellectual property rights including patents. In FY2016, Japan's 86 national universities were divided into three categories: (1) 16 universities that "promote outstanding education and research on par with the world's top universities," consisting mainly of former Imperial Universities; (2) 15 universities that "promote outstanding education and research in many fields through the formation of networks;" and (3) 55 universities that "promote human resource development and research that met regional needs." Japanese national universities were accustomed to dependence on government funding, and they sought this funding by meticulously adhering to the Key Performance Index (KPI) of the Ministry of Education, Culture, Sports, Science and Technology (MEXT), which emphasized industry-academia collaboration. Since then, MEXT-led national university reforms have been implemented, including the 2017 Designated National University and the 2023 Global University of Excellence, but there has been no improvement in the research and innovation creation capabilities of Japanese research universities (Toyoda, 2019). A careful analysis and evaluation, from a global perspective, is needed to determine whether Japan's university policies are truly conducive to facilitating the construction of high-tech industries based on knowledge-based digital-technology.

14 While current MEXT policies promote, perhaps excessively, the for-profit status even after 2003, when national universities were incorporated, by expanding academia-industry collaborations, in the late 1990s, the Ministry of Education (MEXT's predecessor) was still concerned about the national universities becoming too involved in industrial policy. The following anecdote exemplifies this concern. In 1997, when Tohoku University sought the approval and budgetary allocation from the Ministry of Education to establish the "New Industry Creation Hatchery Center (NICHe)," an academia-industry collaborative R&D facility styled on the UIRCs in the United States, the Ministry of Education refused to use the words "New Industry Creation" in the Japanese title of the center. Therefore, the Japanese name was changed to "Future Science and Technology" which seemed less obtrusive, although the English name remained the same. Thus, NICHe, the academia-industry collaborative R&D center for creating breakthrough technological innovation for high-tech industry, has a title that has different meanings in Japanese and English (NICHe, 2019).

15 In April 1982, JAFCO (a leading VC since the early 1970s backed mainly by Nomura Securities Co. Ltd.) introduced the VC Investment Fund modeled after the American Limited Partnership Fund (LPs), enabling Japanese VCs to raise their own investment funds, resulting in a VC boom in the early 1980s. However, in Japan at that time, there was no meaningful academia-industry R&D collaboration and as a result generated very few tech-based startups with high investment-readiness.

16 Foster and Kaplan (2001) classified Private Equity Investors into VC firms that invest in the startup stage and the principal investing firms that invest in the later

stage. VCs are responsible for initial financing of disruptive technologies important to the "creative destruction" called for by Schumpeter, while the principal investing firms are responsible for later stage financing. Both type organizations are needed for innovation creation and creative destruction. For example, as discussed in Chapter 1, it was the principal investing firms, represented by Kohlberg Kravis Roberts (KKR), that were responsible for the deconstructed pursued by Reaganomics.

17 After World War II, Japan adopted a policy of allocating funds through indirect financing to foster the growth of its Fordist-style industries for postwar reconstruction and development. A hierarchical financial structure was adopted, with the Bank of Japan at the top and quasi-governmental financial institutions, city banks, regional banks, "shinkin banks," and credit unions providing funds for policy implementation (Kohama & Watanabe, 1996). However, as the private and public equity markets boomed in the bubble economy, medium-sized companies in the service sector were able to leverage equity finance to accelerate their growth. Under these financial market changes, Japanese VCs functioned as the principal investing firms in growing mid-capitalization companies.

18 To counter the sharp appreciation of the yen, Japan's central government undertook massive monetary easing and fiscal spending. However, while large-scale capital investment in the manufacturing sector was curbed, and capital investment in the nonmanufacturing sector was expanded, the strong yen's recession-proof measures created excess liquidity, leading to speculation in stocks and land, creating a bubble economy which brought about the first domestic demand-driven growth in the Japanese economy, leading to a prolonged economic boom. As a result, the maintenance and expansion of existing industries that relied on physical-based technology became a priority (Economic Planning Agency, 1997).

19 Since the Meiji Restoration, Japan had pursued the "Policy of Enriching and Strengthening the Military" under a strong centralized authoritarian state, aiming to catch up with and surpass the Western powers. While the military-state collapsed with Japan's defeat in World War II, the centralized government reshaped itself with the new national goal to pursue economic wealth as exhibited by the United States (Economic Planning Agency, 1997). As emphasized in this manuscript, successful implementation of the "Technopolis Policy" required the establishment of "Small i" institutions through a shift from the central government-led approach to local initiatives. In Japan, where there were no Silicon Valley success stories, the need for "Capital I" institutions could be envisioned, while the need for establishing "Small i" institutions was not considered.

References

Berman, E. P. (2012). *Creating the Market University*. Princeton, NJ: Princeton University Press.

Best, M. (2001). *The New Competitive Advantage*. Oxford: Oxford University Press.

Botkin, J. W. (1988). "Route 128: Its History and Destiny," pp. 117–123, in R. W. Smilor, G. Kozmetsky, & D. V. Gibson (Eds.), *Creating Technopolis: Linking Technology Commercialization and Economic Development*. Cambridge, UK: Ballinger.

Boutillier, S., D. Carre & N. Levratto (2016). *Entrepreneurial Ecosystems*. Hoboken, NJ, Wiley. ISBN: 978-1-848-21875-8.

Brezis, E. S. & P. R. Krugman (1997). "Technology and the Life Cycle of Cities," *Journal of Economic Growth*, No. 2, 369–383, Kluwer Academic Publisher.

Brinkley, J. (1997). *Defining Vision: The Battle for the Future of Television.* Boston, MA: Houghton Mifflin.

Bygrave, W. D. & J. A. Timmons (1992). *Venture Capital at the Crossroads.* Boston, MA: Harvard Business School Press.

Castells, M. & P. Hall (1994). *Technopolises of the World: The Making of 21st Century Industrial Complexes.* Milton Park, UK: Routledge.

Cavallo, A., A. Ghezzi & R. Balocco (2019). "Entrepreneurial Ecosystem Research: Present Debates and Future Directions," *International Entrepreneurship and Management Journal,* 15. 10.1007/s11365-018-0526-3.

Dorfman, N. S. (1988). "Route 128: The Development of a Regional High Technology Economy," pp. 240–274, in D. Lampe (Ed.), *The Massachusetts Miracle: High Technology and Economic Revitalization.* Boston, MA: MIT Press.

Economic Planning Agency (Ed.) (1997). *The Postwar Japanese Economy* (in Japanese). Ministry of Finance Printing Bureau.

Etzkowitz, H. (1996). "Beyond the Frontier: The Convergence of Military and Civilian R&D in the United States," pp. 119–135, in P. Gummett, M. Boutoussv, J. Farkas & A. Rip (Eds.), *Military R&D after the Cold War.* Norwell, MA: Kluwer Academic Publishers.

Etzkowitz, H. (2002). *MIT and the Rise of Entrepreneurial Science.* Milton Park, UK: Routledge.

Florida, R. & M. Kenney (1990). *The Break-through Illusion: Corporate America's Failure to Move from Innovation to Mass Production.* New York: BasicBooks.

Foss, L. & D. V. Gibson, eds. (2015). *The Entrepreneurial University: Context and Institutional Change.* Milton Park, UK: Routledge.

Foster, R. & S. Kaplan (2001). *Creative Destruction: Why Companies that Are Built to Last Underperform the Market, and How to Successfully Transform Them.* New York: Currency/Doubleday.

Geiger, R. L. (2004). *Research & Relevant Knowledge.* New Brunswick, NJ: Transaction Publishers.

Gibson, D. V. & E. M. Rogers (1994). *R&D Collaboration on Trial: The Microelectronics and Computer Technology Corporation.* Boston, MA: Harvard Business School Press.

Gibson, D. V., G. Kozmetsky & R. W. Smilor, eds. (1992). *The Technopolis Phenomenon: Smart Cities, Fast Systems, Global Networks.* Lanham, MD: Rowan & Littlefield.

Gupta, U. eds. (2004). *The First Venture Capitalist.* Calgary: Gondolier.

Ito, T. (1998). *The Study of Technopolis Policy in Japan* [in Japanese]. Tokyo: Nihon Hyoron-sha.

Jacobs, J. (1969). *The Economy of Cities.* Westminster, London: Penguin Books.

Kenney, M. eds. (2000). *Understanding Silicon Valley.* Stanford, CA: Stanford University Press.

Kohama, H. & M. Watanabe (1996). *Economic Development in Postwar Japan* [in Japanese]. Tokyo: Nihon-Hyoronsha.

Lampe, D. (Ed.) (1988). *The Massachusetts Miracle: High Technology and Economic Revitalization.* Boston, MA: MIT Press.

Leslie, S. W. (1993). *The Cold War and American Science: The Military-Industrial-Academic Complex at MIT and Stanford.* New York: Columbia University Press.

Mallaby, S. (2022). *The Power Law: Venture Capital and the Art of Disruption.* Westminster, UK: Penguin Books.

NICHe, Ed. (2019). *NICHe 20th Anniversary History*. Japan: Tohoku University.

Nicholas, T. (2019). *VC: An American History*. Cambridge, MA: Harvard University Press.

Nishizawa, A. (2009). "Evolution of Japanese-style Venture Capital and Its Limitation: Why Non-liner VC Model Emerged in Japan," *International Journal of Entrepreneurship and Innovation Management*, 9(4), 416–436.

Oftedal, E. M., Dick-Forde, E., & Longsworth, L. (2022). "Activist Leadership in the Caribbean: The Case of the University of West Indies" in T. Iakovleva et al. (Eds.), *Universities and Regional Engagement: From the Exceptional to the Everyday*. London: Routledge.

Powell, W. W., K. Packalen & K. Whittington (2012). "Organizational and Institutional Genesis," pp. 434–465, in J. F. Padgett and W. W. Powell (Eds.), *The Emergence of Organizations and Markets*. Princeton, NJ: Princeton University Press.

Preer, R. W. (1992). *The Emergence of Technopolis: Knowledge-Intensive Technologies and Regional Development*. Westport, CT: Praeger.

Rifkin, G., & Harrar, G. (1990). *The Ultimate Entrepreneur*. Rocklin, CA: Prima Publishing & Communications.

Romer, P. M. (1992). "Two Strategies for Economic Development: Using Ideas and Producing Ideas," pp. 63–91, in L. H. Summers & S. Shah (Eds.), *Proceedings of the World Bank Annual Conference on Development Economics*. Washington DC, World Bank.

Rosenbloom, R. S. & W. J. Spencer (1996). *Engines of Innovation*. Boston, MA: HBS Press.

Smilor, R., D. Gibson & G. Kozmetsky (1988). "Creating the Technopolis: High Technology Development in Austin, Texas," *Journal of Business Venturing*, 4(1), 49–67.

Storper, M. (2013). *Keys to the City: How Economics, Institutions, Social Interactions, and Politics Shape Development*. Princeton, NJ: Princeton University Press.

Suzuki, S. (2001). *Research on High-tech Development Policies* (in Japanese). London, UK: Minerva.

Tatsuno, S. (1986). *The Technopolis Strategy: Japan, High Technology, and the Control of the Twenty-First Century*. Upper Saddle River, NJ: Brady Book.

Tarui, Y. & The Semiconductor Industry Newspaper eds. (2000). *The Chronicle of Japanese Semiconductor Industry 1948–1999 [in Japanese]*. Tokyo: Industry Times Corporation.

Terdiman, D., "How NASA Helped Invent Silicon Valley, Staff Writer," CNET News.com, October 2, 2007.

Toyoda, N. (2019). *Crisis of Scientific Nation* (in Japanese). Tokyo: Toyo-keizai Shinposha.

Tsusho Sangyo Sho (1980). *The Vision of MITI Policies in 1980s: Summary* (in Japanese). Tokyo: MITI Information Office.

Warsh, D. (2006). *Knowledge and the Wealth of Nations: A Story of Economic Discovery*. Manhattan, NY: Norton.

3 Technology Venturing and Theoretical Modeling for "New Capital I" and "New Small i" Institutions

This chapter explores our designated theoretical background clarifying why and how (1) institutions can facilitate endogenous, technology-based economic development; (2) "New Capital I" and "New Small i" institutions are formed and sustained; and (3) "robust actors" play a critical role in building "New Small i" institutions. These theories are used as an analytical lens, in Chapter 4, to elucidate the generalizability of our observations of our comparative analysis of Austin, Texas, and Tsuruoka, Japan.

1 The Digital Technological Revolution and "New Capital I" Institutions

Regarding the need for building new institutions for innovative economic development, Helpman (2004, p. 140) observed that institutions that "are good for one period in time, are not necessarily good for another" because the emergence of new technologies motivates the need for institutions that are compatible with the new technologies. In this regard, Perez (2002) presents a useful model for elucidating the staged development process of capitalism by linking "Technological Revolutions" with institutional transformation. Perez notes an important turning point evoked by the divergence of "financial capital" from real capital or "production capital" and the incompatibility between new technology and existing institutions. She also stipulates that the staged development of capitalism from the industrial age toward the end of the 18th century to the 21st century has resulted in five "Technological Revolutions."[1] She defines the present age as a transformation period from Fordist-style mass production brought by dthe fourth technological revolution to the fifth revolution of microelectronics technology fundamental to information and telecommunication industries.

However, Perez's emphasis on deriving a model that is adaptable to staged capitalism development seems to prevent her from making a clear distinction between analogue technology of the industrial age and digital microelectronics technology. As a result, "the Age of Information and Telecommunications," which began in the early 1970s, exhibits a different transition from the Perez model. According to Perez, the "dot-com bubble burst" of 2000 was an

DOI: 10.4324/9781003488149-4

important turning point,[2] after which came the "Deployment" phase. While we appreciate Perez's suggestion that the staged development of capitalism was accompanied by a transition of institutions evoked by "Technological Revolutions," we suggest that instead of the synergy depicted by Perez, we see the fragmentation of regions and hierarchies resulting in the financial crisis of 2008 and the formation of high-tech industries based on digital technology that required contradictory policy responses.

As described in Chapter 1, in the early 1980s, in an attempt to rescue the US economy from stagflation, Reaganomics was composed of two contradicting policy perspectives: one focused on deregulation and market fundamentalism, and the other focused on "Industrial Innovation Policy" which introduced new macro institutions to foster conditions that encouraged the formation of high-tech industrial clusters and the commercialization of disruptive innovations. As a result of this apparent contradiction, the Reagan administration was resistant to officially support the implementation of "Industrial Innovation Policy" which was based on the vision outlined in Vannevar Bush's *Science, the Endless Frontier: A Report to the President* (Washington. D.C., 1945). However, "Industrial Innovation Policy" was formally recognized and supported by the Bush administration in that the Bayh-Dole Act and the Stevenson-Wydler Act profoundly affected private-sector research and development (R&D) by encouraging cooperation across academic and public sectors. According to Cohen and Delong (2016), academia-industry-government (AIG) collaborative R&D established by "Industrial Innovation Policy" was historically unprecedented. Link and Cunningham (2021, p. 8) state that AIG collaborative R&D played an important and complementary role to private-sector R&D. The Economic Recovery Tax Act, the Small Business Innovation Development Act, and the National Cooperative Research Act of 1984 were all important in the commercialization of market-changing technologies resulting from AIG collaborative R&D. However, Link and Cunningham (2021) did not describe how to commercialize market-changing technologies emerging from AIG collaborative R&D, and this deficit becomes evident when comparing their framework defining technology policy to one referring to "New Capital I" institutions as depicted in Figure 3.1.

While Link and Cunningham (2021) noted the importance of Small Business Innovation Research (SBIR), they did not identify other necessary policy initiatives such as the introduction of private equity markets (PEMs) for facilitating investments in tech-based startups by business angels, venture capitalists (VCs), and other private equity investors along with expanding emerging capital markets symbolized by NASDAQ to activate and expand private equity investors' investments. Technology policy as described by Link and Cunningham (2021) does not include building PEMs to facilitate private equity investments needed to support regional startups and their continued growth. The federal government's "Industrial Innovation Policy" was formulated and implemented to not only induce technological innovation but also to change "R&D, technology, and innovation processes" as clearly noted by

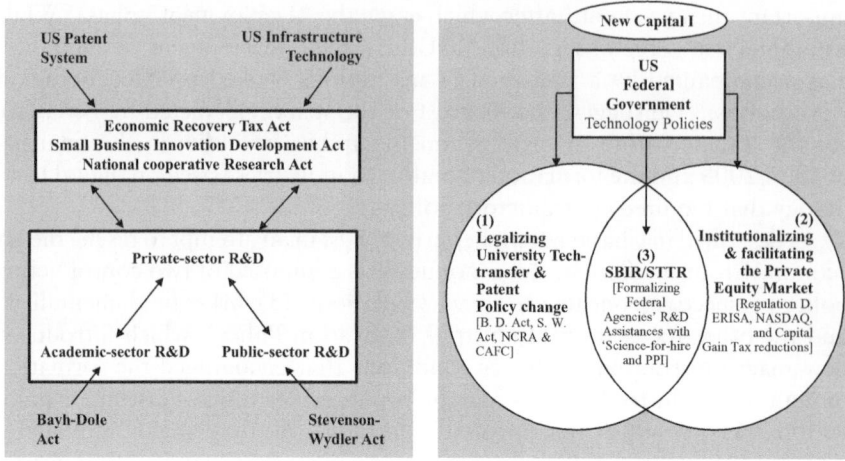

Figure 3.1 The US "Technology Policy": Different Frameworks from Different Perspectives

Source: Reproduced Figure 1.2 from Link and Cunningham (2021)

Link and Cunningham (2021, p. 6). Tech-based startups were expected to play crucial roles in these innovation processes; therefore, a new investment market called PEM was necessary for financial support. As referenced in Chapter 2, American Research and Development (ARD), the world's first VC firm providing financial support to tech-based startups, and Digital Equipment Corporation (DEC) were essential players to the building Boston R128.

Digitally based high-tech industries were largely the result of disruptive innovations brought by the commercialization of key market-changing technologies that emerged not from R&D in large firms but from AIG collaborative R&D and the agglomeration of tech-based startups, many of which were launched from military R&D (Turner, 2006). Digital technology was a disruptive technology in part because, unlike analog technology in which it is possible to recognize technical problems through visual and other means, digital technology needed to be analyzed and composed in complex codes to solve problems.[3] In order to implement digital technology, 'use-inspired basic research' is important to realizing technology needs at the bit level to enable coding. The Department of Defense (DOD) invited the participation of universities through the "military-industrial-academic complex" leading to AIG contributing to the manufacture of new weapons using digital technology. However, AIG also facilitated DOD's collaborative R&D toward digital technology applications for civilian use outside the military. Etzkowitz (2002, p. 16) called the innovative entrepreneurial university and the Bayh-Dole Act as a "second 'land grant'" transformation.

Freeman (1986) modeled tech-based startups creating disruptive innovations based on Schumpeter's (1942) Mark I model of entrepreneurial innovation requiring AIG collaborative R&D as contrasted with Schumpeter's Mark II model of large-firm-managed innovation system where the critical role was played by central research institutes belonging to large firms as shown in Figure 3.2. [4]

An important challenge is that disruptive innovations created under Mark I innovation systems require high-risk funding as they initially realize low rates of return on investments when compared with Mark II large-firm-based incremental innovations. The lower initial profitability expected for private-sector investments under Mark I R&D innovation systems is the result of high risk in commercializing market-changing technologies emerging from digital-based technological inventions through the "exogenous science and invention" of universities and federal labs. "Thus, there is a strong consensus that, in absence of government intervention, there would be underinvestment in R&D in free market economies." In short, "innovation market failures exist and government initiatives can alleviate them" (Link & Siegel, 2007, p. 170).

The DOD encouraged the transition from Mark II to Mark I innovation systems by leveraging "the military-industrial-academic complex," as discussed in Chapter 2, and to exploit the benefits brought by the innovation creation system advocated by V. Bush's *Science: The Endless Frontier* (Cohen & Delong, 2016). In an effort to reduce business risks of Mark I innovation systems and to exploit the benefits brought by digital technologies for military requirements after World War II, the DOD (1) funded initiatives for "use-inspired basic research" under "military-industrial-academic complex" by clarifying commercialization targets and specifications for

Mark I : Schumpeter's model of Entrepreneurial Innovation

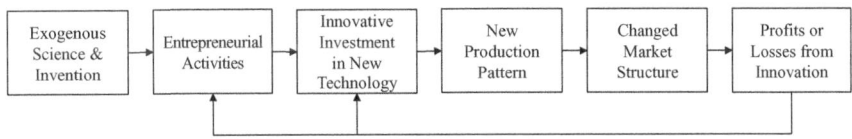

Mark II : Schumpeter's model of Large-firm Managed Innovation

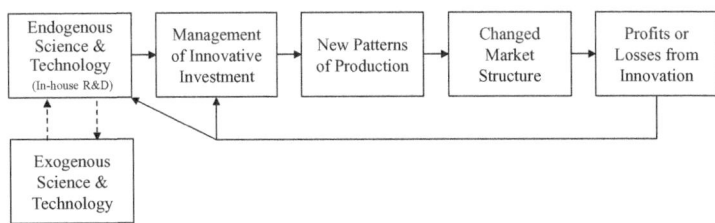

Figure 3.2 Schematic Representation of Schumpeter Mark I and II

Source: Freeman (1982, pp. 212–213)

universities, (2) worked to push academia's "use-inspired basic research" results to be commercialized by tech-based startups, and (3) worked to establish supporting measures enabling tech-based startups to play critical roles in commercializing digital-based breakthrough technologies (Cohen & Delong, 2016). DOD introduced new institutions including cost-plus payments to enable tech-based startups to carry out business plans even at an early stage of R&D instead of the traditional governmental subsidiary of matching grants (Wessner, 1999).[5] DOD also promoted "science-for-hire" to enable collaborative R&D between tech-based startups and entrepreneurial universities (Servo, 2005, p. 27) and started "public procurement for innovation (PPI)" enabling prototypes with functioning "minimum viable products (MVPs)" to be purchased by the government (Weiss, 2014).[6]

As noted after World War II, the DOD actively intervened to transpose its military technological R&D innovation system from Mark II to Mark I by helping to build new innovation supporting institutions. However, Fordist-style mass-manufacturing industries under the Mark II innovation system were still the dominant industry model, having brought economic prosperity to Detroit and many other US regions during the 1950s and 1960s. Furthermore, there was a strong US tradition of favoring private initiative and avoiding federal intervention as much as possible. Therefore, initially DOD's Mark I model was generally limited to military technological R&D and did not expand to commercial high-tech industries in regions beyond Boston R128 and Silicon Valley (Miller & Côté, 1987). To save the US economy from stagflation, DOD's Mark I model needed to be expanded to a range of federal government agencies, to disseminate systems for creating disruptive innovations where tech-based startups played a critical role in commercializing market-changing technologies emerging from AIG collaborative R&D. Accordingly, toward the end of the 1970s and the early 1980s, the US federal government's "Industrial Innovation Policy" became an important trigger for building "New Capital I" institutions in an effort to catalyze Silicon Valley-type high-tech industrial clusters across the United States.

In summary, "New Capital I" institutions played critical roles in transposing the US innovation system from Mark II to Mark I. These institutional changes were essential in realizing a technology paradigm shift from physical-based analogue technology to knowledge-based digital technology. Yet these "New Capital I" institutions were not sufficient, in themselves, to realize the launch and growth of regionally based high-tech industries (Storper, 2013).

2   Technology Venturing and "New Small i" Institutions

With time, tech-based startups became increasingly recognized as being key to commercializing disruptive innovations and market-changing technologies emerging from AIG collaborative R&D. However, numerous and serious business risks inhibited tech-based startups from bridging between universities and markets under Mark I innovation systems. Kozmetsky et al. (1985, p. 82) categorized the disruptive innovation creating process as "Technology Venturing" under Mark I innovation systems meaning "the process by which major institutions took and shared risk in integrating and commercializing scientific research and technologies."

"New Capital I" institutions—formulated and implemented by national "Industrial Innovation Policy" toward the end of the 1970s and early 1980s—motivated necessary change in industrial policies of state governments. Before 1980, state governments tended to induce industry recruitment with "supply side" policy models which focused on infrastructure development and preferential taxation to create low-cost business environments. "Industrial Innovation Policy" encouraged state governments to move from "supply side" to "demand side" industrial initiatives, which focused on providing financial and other necessary support to tech-based startups (Eisinger, 1988, pp. 10–12). However, while state governments expanded policies to provide risk money for tech-based startups, there were still crucial expertise gaps in "Early-stage Technology Development (ESTD)" that were not amenable to solutions from top-down policies. Disruptive innovations which emerged under Schumpeter's Mark I innovation system were often not supported by established large companies as it could take up to ten years or more to realize concrete results and to earn a profit. Indeed, the policies adopted by many states to financially support tech-based start-ups ended in failure (Eisinger, 1988, pp. 245–249). As a result, meaningful Technology Venturing support was often difficult to attain from existing regional academic, business, and government sectors. As noted in the evolution of Boston R128, it took years before the support measures for tech-based startups—as proposed by Flanders, Compton, Doriot—were able to revitalize the regional economy (Etzkowitz, 2002).

As noted, disruptive innovation development processes under the Mark I innovation system are inherently high risk, especially in ESTD; accordingly, tech-based startups benefit from the support of regional institutions through public and private entities' networking to share these risks. The Sequential model shown in Figure 3.3 illustrates the specifics of high risk in ESTD (Branscomb & Auerswald, 2002). As depicted, one inherent risk factor is that funding is likely to not be available for ESTD—the critical phase in which both basic and applied research is developed concurrently.

In ESTD, R&D priorities need to undergo major shifts from university's "use-inspired basic research" to applied research for market development. When use-inspired basic research in the Invention stage results in a market-changing technology, money providers seek a "Proof of Concept (POC)" to clarify the technology's validity, and a patent application is often needed to protect inventions with industrial applicability. In this transition from research to development, the creation of prototypes (with specific function for the candidate market) becomes a critical target. In ESTD, tech-based startups must concurrently complete two important steps of prototyping

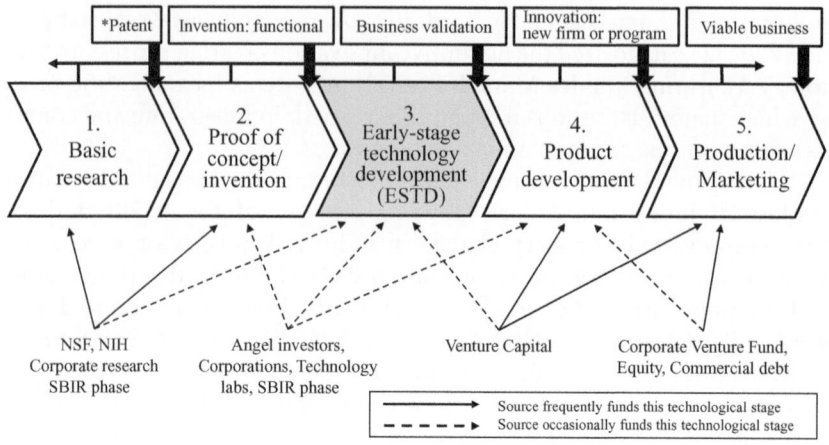

Figure 3.3 Sequential Model of Development and Funding

*A more complete model would address the fact that patents occur throughout the process.

Note: The region corresponding to early-stage technology development is shaded in gray. The boxes at top indicate milestones in the development of a science-based innovation. The arrows across the top of, and in between, the five stages represented in this sequential model are intended to suggest the many complex ways in which the stages interrelate. Multiple exit options are available to technology entrepreneurs at different stages in this branching sequence of events.

Source: Branscomb & Auerwald (2002, p. 33)

and business validation. Reduction to practice and prototyping embodies the patented POC key market-changing technology in a Minimum Viable Product (MVP), while business validation requires clarification of the prototype's marketability and profitability.

The inherent risks in prototyping (technical risk) and business validation (market risk) are increased by the need to complete these two steps concurrently (Servo, 2005). Therefore, tech-based startups responsible for implementing ESTD can be categorized as "minus two stage companies," exhibiting higher risk when compared to typical startups as shown in Figure 3.3 (Shane, 2005). Market failure occurs when investors cannot effectively assess risk and return (Tassey, 1997).[7] Such market failures are so common they are described as the "Valley of Death" that separates R&D from the marketplace (Branscomb & Auerswald, 2002). For tech-based startups to overcome the "Valley of Death" and bridge the gap between R&D and markets, it is essential to secure risk money such as SBIR, angel investors, or venture capital. Importantly, while risk money providers are viewed as a necessary component of "New Capital I" institutions, they are not sufficient, as tech-based startups also need value-added management support and advice to successfully implement ESTD.

Effective business incubator services provide more than physical infrastructure and "hardware apparatus" as a physical operating site; perhaps more importantly, they also provide "software" management support services in addition to monetary and human resources (Miller & Côté, 1987; Kalis, 2001; Wiggins & Gibson, 2003). Auerswald and Branscomb (2003) categorize such software management support services as being provided through the "collective entrepreneurship" of external champions who take and share the vison and risks of the tech-based startup entrepreneurs. Research also emphasizes the importance of relational networks connecting funding agencies, private equity investors, and external champions to enable business incubators to fulfill needed supporting functions. Furthermore, we suggest that to realize successful technology venturing, it is necessary to build specialized actor-networks based on the principle of "give before you get" rather than the market principle of "give and take." Feld (2012, p. 111) notes that investors and external champions can play important roles in "building winners" with the principle of "give before you get," as it enables tech-based startups housed in business incubators to implement ESTD through taking and sharing risks. Storper (2013) categorized these actor-networks connecting funding agencies, private equity investors, external champions, and professional support as "Small i" institutions.

Many studies that have attempted to clarify Silicon Valley's development from the perspective of institutional theory most investigated the structure of the new institutions defined as actor-networks rather than clarifying their institutionalization processes.[8] Indeed, in response to such studies, Scott (2014, pp. 256–257) noted that institutionalizing processes are perhaps more important than structural investigation, and he suggests the challenge for institutional theory in the 21st century lies in clarifying the processes of changing institutions in contemporary capitalism.

3   "New Small i" Institutionalization Processes

As previously noted, North defined institutions as "the rules of the game in society or, more formally, the humanly devised constraints that shape human interaction… to reduce uncertainty by establishing stable (but not necessarily efficient) structures for human interaction," and these constraints "are the underlying determinant of the long-run performance of economies" (North, 1990, pp. 3–6, 107). Formal constraints can be identified by laws and regulations, whereas informal constraints emerge through social conventions and behavioral norms. North placed considerable weight in the importance of informal constraints as he noted that the premeditated change of institutions is impossible due to imperviousness of informal constraints emerging from conventions and norms of people's behavior. Both types of constraints—formal and informal—can have mutually complementary characteristics, but they may not always be mutually supportive. While formal constraints tend to change discontinuously by "revolution and conquest," institutions tend to change incrementally since informal constraints can deter discontinuous institutional change (North, 1990, p. 6). North continued that while "the difference between informal and formal constraints is one of degree," institutional change cannot occur without being linked to formal and informal constraints simultaneously due to their complementarity (North, 1990, p. 46).

In alignment with North's (1990) theoretical perspective, Storper considers informal constraints as central to "Small i," mezzo-level institutions, as the economic development of cities is heavily constrained by "organizations of the key 'groups' or 'communities' in the economy." He identifies informal constraints imposed by "the organization of key 'groups' or 'communities' in the economy while noting that "Small i" institutions can be an important bridge between "Capital I" macro-level institutions and micro level activities (Storper, 2013, p. 8), see Table 3.1.

Storper states that tech-based economic growth benefits from disruptive innovations realized through appropriate "Small i" institutions. He notes, for example, that "Small i" institutions were important to forming Silicon Valley and US regional biotech clusters under "norms of openness, and cross-domain network connections" (Storper, 2013, pp. 129, 136). These activities and connections required transposition from "Existing Small i" to "New Small i" institutions that could support tech-based startups and enable them to grow as "anchor tenants" (initial success firms)—making it possible to launch additional high-tech companies, leading to technology industry growth through the regional agglomeration of anchor tenants and support organizations.

Table 3.1 Hierarchical Classification of Institutions and Drivers and Challenges of Institutional Transformation

Hierarchical Classification of Institutions	*Definitions*		*Drivers of Conversion*	*Challenges of Conversion*
"Capital I" institutions	Macro institutions at national and state levels implement formal policies backed by laws and regulations.		Tech development and revolutions "institutions that are good for one period are not necessarily good in another" (Helpman, 2004, p. 140). This dissonance motivates institutional change to better accommodate the needs of emerging technologies	A key issue facing institutional conversion is motivations to protect the vested interests of existing institutions threatened by "Political Creative Destruction" evoked by institutional conversion (Acemoglu et al., 2019, p. 583).
"Small i" institutions	Mezzo institutions at the regional level, formed and implemented through regional governmental policies or local actor initiatives reinforced by normative and cultural-cognitive behavior	Institutional Conversion from Existing to New		

Source: Authors

Scott also emphasizes the importance of "anchor tenants" in the creation of industry clusters. Broadening Storper's (2013) characterization of "anchor tenants" as being "initial successful firms," Scott refers to anchor tenants as being "able to generate new types of organizations," "hybrid forms" that permit "boundary crossing," and "the mixing of institutional logics and practices that allow for the translation of ideas from one realm, basic science, to another, the creation of commercial products" (Scott, 2014, p. 250). Scott contends that "anchor tenants" play a critical role in creating 21st-century high-tech industries where Fordist-style, vertically integrated organizations are decomposed in favor of a variety of networked forms and flexible commodity- and value-chain production systems (Scott, 2014, pp. 250–251). Thus, over time, "anchor tenants" and "New Small i" institutions that supplement "New Capital I" institutions enable a technological paradigm shift across an industry.

The status quo of existing institutions is defined by DiMaggio and Powell (1983) as an "iron cage" where "robust actors" are essential to building successful "New Small i" institutions.[9] Storper (2013) also emphasizes the importance of "robust actors" who build and support "New Small i" institutions accompanied by a "transposition of norms."[10] Storper concludes that Silicon Valley's initial burst in high-tech economic development was, in large part, the result of the actions of "robust actors" such as Frederick Terman, William Shockley, Gordon Moore, Robert Noyce, Bill Hewlett, David Packard, Stewart Brand, Alf Heller, Steve Jobs, researchers at Xerox Parc, and a host of others (Storper, 2013, p. 135). Interestingly, Frederick Terman, commonly referred to as the Godfather of Silicon Valley, studied under Vannevar Bush at MIT before becoming professor and dean of the School of Engineering and ultimately provost at Stanford University.[11]

We suggest that Scott's "Organizational Field Model" provides a useful theoretical lens to analyze where "actors" play critical roles in institutionalizing processes (see Figure 3.4). Having identified the three pillars of institutions at regulative, normative, and cultural-cognitive levels of analysis (please refer to Figure 0.2), Scott (2014) offers a model of "top-down and bottom-up" processes of institutional creation and diffusion.

The concept of organization field expands the framework of analytic attention to encompass relevant actors, institutional logistics, and governance structures that empower and constrain the actions of participants – both individuals and organizations – in a delimited social sphere. It includes within its purview all of the parties that are meaningfully involved in some collective enterprise – whether producing a product or service, carrying out some specific policy, or attempting to resolve a common issue. The concept has not only encouraged attention to a "higher" (more encompassing) level of analysis; it has stimulated interest in organizational processes that take place over longer periods of time. To adequately comprehend the determinants,

Figure 3.4 Top-Down and Bottom-Up Processes of Institutional Creation and Diffusion

Source: Scott (2014, p. 237)

> mechanisms, and effects of significant institutional change – or stability
> for that matter – demands attention to longer periods of time
>
> (Scott, 2014: 258)

Scott defines organizational fields as a community of organizations that partakes of a common meaning system and whose participants interact more frequently and fatefully with one another than with actors outside of the field. Less concerned with explaining the sources of bureaucracy, Scott highlights the relational nature of the interactions within fields and how shared understandings of a situation bind organizations to one another (Wooten, 2015). In short, Scott emphasizes "Collective Rationality" over institutional "Isomorphism" as presented by DiMaggio and Powell (1983) in "The Iron Cage Revisited: Institutional Isomorphism and Collective Rationality in Organizational Fields" which focuses on how institutions strongly constrain personal actions. Scott (2014) accepts the potential for individual actors to transform institutions as they acquire "Collective Rationality" through negotiations in an organization field of activity. Scott's "top down and bottom-up" processes of institutionalization and diffusion highlight the interactivity and influence of individual actors and social institutions surrounding governance structures and organizations.[12] He places this "Collective Rationality" as the core of acquiring social legitimacy and establishing new cultural-cognitive, normative, and even regulative pillars.

Scott proposes the "Three Pillars of Institutionalization" and the Organization Field Model as generalizable theoretical concepts applicable to broad cases of establishing and transforming institutions. Scott indicates that even national-level institutions (in our reasoning "Capital I" institutions) built by laws and regulations are not fully embedded as macro institutions without establishing normative and cultural-cognitive pillars. To demonstrate the validity of institutionalization processes in building "New Small i" institutions, Scott (2014) states that it is necessary to identify the appropriate organization field. This can be a challenging task when looking at different contexts while clarifying the specifics of institution building. Yet we believe that this limitation may be addressed by referring to the Organization Field Model as generalizable in the building of "New Small i" institutions in reducing and sharing risks for successful technology venturing at regulative, normative, and culturally cognitive levels of analysis.

In Chapter 4, we explore the generalizability of these concepts through the comparative cases of Austin, Texas, and Tsuruoka, Japan. In the Austin case, we describe important events and the activities of robust actors that contributed to Austin's exceptional technology-based entrepreneurial growth beginning in the mid-1980s. We highlight specific "historical trigger events" that motivated the formation of new "Small i institutions" linking government, business, and academic sectors in successful technology firm recruitment and regionally based technology venturing. In comparison, we describe the "Miracle of Tsuruoka" in which a tech-based startup served as a "trigger" to establish supporting "New Small i" institutions that initiated regional tech-based growth that had been long sought through Japan's failed Technopolis Policy and "Cloning Silicon Valley Policy." We compare the causations of these transformational successes—in spite of disparate cultural regions, national contexts, and policies—to clarify the role of "influencers" who create initiatives and enable new "Small i" institutions by "invention" and "negotiation" in an "Organization Field" of activity.

Notes

1 Perez classifies the gradual development of the capitalist economy from the 1770s to the 2000s through the technological revolution into five stages as follows: first, the "Industrial Revolution" initiated by "Arkwright's mill that opened in Cromford in 1771; second, the "Age of Steam and Railways" and "Test of the 'Rocket' steam engine for the Liverpool-Manchester railway" in 1829; third, the "Age of Steel, Electricity and Heavy Engineering" and "The Carnegie Bessemer steel plant that opens in Pittsburgh, Pennsylvania" in 1875; fourth, the "Age of Oil, the Automobile and Mass Production" and "First Model-T comes out of the Ford plant in Detroit, Michigan" in 1908; and fifth, the "Age of Information

and Telecommunications" when "The Intel microprocessor is announced in Santa Clara, California" in 1971 (Perez, 2002, p. 11).

2   Due to the limitations of the date of her publication, we note that Perez (2002) did not mention the inevitability of the "Age of Information and Telecommunications" based on digitalized microelectronics without focusing on the "Technological Revolution," which should be categorized as an important technological paradigm shift from analogue to digital.

3   A similar technological revolution occurred in life sciences with the discovery that "instructions for building every cell in every form of life were encoded by the four-letter sequences of DNA giving birth to an information age based on digital coding (i.e., 010011) and genetic coding (i.e., ACTG)" (Issacson, 2022, p. 28).

4   The field of entrepreneurship theory owes much to J. Schumpeter's (1883–1950) contributions. His fundamental theories are often referred to as Mark I and Mark II. In Mark I, Schumpeter argued that the innovation and technological change of a nation come from entrepreneurs or wild spirits and asserted that "... the doing of new things or the doing of things that are already being done in a new way" stemmed directly from the efforts of entrepreneurs. However, in supporting Mark II, Schumpeter argued that the agents that drive innovation and the economy are large companies that have the capital to invest in R&D of new products and services and to deliver them to customers more cheaply, thus raising their standard of living *Capitalism, Socialism, and Democracy* by Joseph Schumpeter (1942).

5   The government often adopts matching grants to support new technology developments in private for-profit companies. However, high risk can make entrepreneurs reluctant to invest personal resources in breakthrough technological R&D. While entrepreneurs should perhaps bear some of this risk (due to the potential for profit provided by matching grants), there seems to be an inherent mandate for the DOD to establish business activities for high-risk breakthrough R&D technologies, due to the potential benefits to the DOD. Therefore, the DOD adopted "cost-plus contracts" to enable tech-based startups to engage in high-risk high-tech breakthrough military R&D (Wessner, 1999, p. 4).

6   DOD prototype purchases perform an earlyvangelist's function. "Earlyvangelists are a special breed of customer willing to take a risk on your startup's product or service because they can envision its potential to solve a critical and immediate problem and they have the budget to purchase it. Unfortunately, most customers don't fit this profile" (Blank, 2013, p. 45). Furthermore, DOD financial engagement can provide a market-signaling effect, "acting as a 'certifier' of promising new technologies," which can be pivotal for breakthrough technology success (Wessner, 2008, p. 19).

7   Knight defines "uncertainty" as a phenomenon that investors cannot evaluate a priori as a random variable and derives the "entrepreneur" concept as a specialized function that overcomes this uncertainty and brings new returns to the society (Knight, 2006).

8   Kenney and Von Burg (2000, pp. 220–229) pointed out that "the essence of Silicon Valley is a set of institutions dedicated to firm creation" and defined this set of institutions as Silicon Valley-specific "Economy Two." They attempted to derive the building of Economy Two from the characteristics of the semiconductor industry. In their explanation, they argue that the semiconductor industry, which grew rapidly due to military demand, brought enormous profits to technology startups and VCs, and that "their success and willingness to invest in new ventures led to path dependence, in the sense of role models and incentives for others to follow norms." Their explanation is the result of an attempt to identify not only the structure of Economy Two but also its institutionalization process. While we share their awareness of the problem, we do not agree with their analysis, which attempts to make institutionalization driven by industry characteristics.

9 Acemoglu et al. (2019) cite "political creative destruction" induced by the transformation from existing institutions to new ones as the reason why the status quo
is so resilient. The authors refer "political creative destruction" to the process by
which economic growth destabilizes existing regimes and reduces the political
power of the "old guard." They conclude that "fear of creative destruction and
political creative destruction makes many rulers ban the adoption of new technologies and block the process of economic development" (p. 583).

10 Storper (2013, p. 134) referenced his reasoning on the importance of "robust
actors" based on "Robust Action and the Rise of the Medici, 1400–1434"
(Padgett and Ansell, 1993), that argue that transformation from existing institutions to new ones is essential when responding to historical crises such as "wars
or fiscal crisis" which force or motivate "robust actors" to overcome pressure to
maintain "preexisting institutions."

11 A seminal event in the development of Silicon Valley was the arrival of celebrated
physicist William Shockley who left Bell Labs and New Jersey, for Northern
California, after helping to develop the transistor which was to become a transformative technology. He founded Shockley Semiconductor in 1955 in Mountain
View, California—in part, to be near his elderly mother who lived in Palo Alto,
the home of Stanford University. The founding of Silicon Valley is often attributed
to the "traitorous eight" a group of engineers Shockley brought with him including Gordon E. Moore and Robert Noyce to work at Shockley Semiconductor
which, for a variety of reasons, became an incubator of considerable talent and
spinoff and startup activity in the Bay Area (Heffernan, 2022). Indeed, led by Bob
Noyce these entrepreneurial engineers left Shockley Semiconductor to found Fairchild Semiconductor in 1957. As excellent examples of "Robust Actors," Moore
and Noyce left Fairchild to found Intel (Integrated electronics) in 1968. With
the support of investor Arthur Rock and the executive leadership and vision of
Andrew Grove, Intel became a key player in the rise of Silicon Valley as a globally
important high-tech center or Technopolis. With large and demanding federal
government customers like NASA (National Aeronautics and Space Administration) Fairchild and Intel became major recipients of government-sponsored projects in the early 1960s just as semiconductor companies were learning how to
design and manufacturer advanced integrated circuits. Referring to Scott (2014,
p. 250) Fairchild Semiconductor and Intel were important anchor tenants for Silicon Valley in generating new types of organizations (e.g. spinout companies) that
led to "boundary crossing," and "the mixing of institutional logics and practices
allowing for the translation of ideas to the creation of commercial products"

12 Scott (2014) insists that socially approved legitimacy is the most important
factor enabling new organization to be institutionalized. Concrete objects and
contents of actors' invention/negotiation in an organization field should be pur-
posed toward acquiring "Collective Rationality" resulting in socially approved
legitimacy. In other words, a dynamic organization field, through which actors
try to enable their disruptive organizations to acquire "Collective Rationality"
through "Constitutive Activities," is visualized as the institutionalization model
showing new institutions embedded into society, thus proving their legitimacy in
an organization field.

References

Acemoglu, D., D. Laibson & J. A. List (2019). *Economics*, 2nd Edition. Harlow, UK:
Pearson.

Auerswald, P. E. & L. M. Branscomb (2003). "Start-ups and Spin-offs," pp. 61–91,
in D. M. Hart (Ed.), *The Emergence of Entrepreneurship Policy: Governance,*

Start-ups and Growth in the U.S. Economy. Cambridge, UK: Cambridge University Press.

Berman, E. P. (2012). *Creating the Market University.* Princeton, NJ: Princeton University Press.

Blank, S. (2013). *The Four Steps to the Epiphany: Successful Strategies for Products that Win,* 5th Edition. K&S Ranch.

Branscomb, L. M. & P. E. Auerswald (Eds.) (2002). *Between Invention and Innovation an Analysis of Funding for Early-Stage Technology Development.* Gaithersburg, MD: Nat'l Institute of Standards and Technology. GCR 02–841.

Cohen, S. S. & J. B. Delong (2016). *Concrete Economics: The Hamilton Approach to Economic Growth and Policy.* Boston, MA: Harvard Business School Press.

DiMaggio, P. J. & W. W. Powell (1983). "The Iron Cage Revisited: Institutional Isomorphism and Collective Rationality in Organizational Fields," pp. 147–160, *American Sociological Review,* 48.

Eisinger, P. K. (1988). *The Rise of the Entrepreneurial State: State and Local Economic Development Policy in the United States.* Madison: University of Wisconsin Press.

Etzkowitz, H. (2002). *MIT and the Rise of Entrepreneurial Science.* London, UK: Routledge.

Feld, B. (2012). *Startup Communities: Building an Entrepreneurial Ecosystem in Your City.* Hoboken, NJ: Wiley & Sons.

Freeman, C. (1986). *The Economics of Industrial Innovation,* 2nd Edition. Cambridge, MA: MIT Press.

Heffernan, V. (2022). "Tiny but Mighty: How the Silicon Chip became the Epicenter of Geopolitical Conflict" in *The New York Times Book Review,* November 20, 2022, p. 12.

Helpman, E. (2004). *The Mystery of Economic Growth.* Cambridge, MA: Harvard University Press.

Issacson, W. (2022). *The Code Breaker: Jennifer Doudna, Gene Editing, and the Future of the Hunan Race.* London: Simon & Schuster Ltd.

Kalis, N. (2001). *Technology Commercialization through New Company Formation: Why US Universities Are Incubating Companies.* Athens, OH: NBIA Publications.

Kenney, M. & U. Von Burg (2000). *Institutions and Economies: Creating Silicon Valley.* Stanford, CA: Stanford University Press.

Knight, F. H. (2006). *Risk, Uncertainty and Profit.* Mineora, NY: Dover Publications.

Kozmetsky, G., M. D. Gill & R. W. Smilor (1985). *Financing and Managing Fast-Growth Companies: The Venture Capital Process.* Lanham, MD: Lexington Books.

Link, A. N. & D. S. Siegel (2007). *Innovation, Entrepreneurship, and Technological Change.* Oxford, UK: Oxford University Press.

Link, A. N. & J. A. Cunningham (2021). *Advanced Introduction to Technology Policy.* Northampton, MA: Edward Elgar.

Miller, C. (2022). *Chip War: The Fight for the World's Most Critical Technology.* New York: Simon and Schuster.

Miller, R. & M. Côté (1987). *Growing the Next Silicon Valley.* Lexington, MA: Lexington Books.

National Research Council (2014). *SBIR at the Department of Defense.* Washington, DC: The National Academies Press. https://doi.org/10.17226/18821

North, D. C. (1990). *Institutions, Institutional Change and Economic Performance.* Cambridge, UK: Cambridge University Press.

Padgett, J. F., & Ansell, C. K. (1993). "Robust Action and the Rise of the Medici, 1400-1434", *American Journal of Sociology* 98, 1259–1319.

Perez, C. (2002). *Technological Revolutions and Financial Capital: The Dynamics of Bubbles and Golden Ages.* Northampton, MA: Edward Elgar.

Schumpeter, J. (1942). *Capitalism, Socialism, and Democracy.* Florence, SC: Taylor & Francis Group. ISBN 978-0-203-85709-0.

Scott, W. R. (2014). *Institutions and Organizations: Ideas, Interests, and Identities,* 4th Edition. Thousand Oaks, CA: SAGE.

Servo, J. C. (2005). *Business Planning for Scientist & Engineers,* 4th Edition. Galveston, TX: Dawnbreaker.

Shane, S. (2005). *Academic Entrepreneurship: Universities Spinoffs and Wealth Creation. New Horizons in Entrepreneurship Series.* Northampton, MA: Edward Elgar.

Storper, M. (2013). *Keys to the City: How Economics, Institutions, Social Interaction, and Politics Shape Development.* Princeton, NJ: Princeton University Press.

Tassey, G. (1997). *The Economics of R&D Policy.* Westport, CT: Quorum.

Turner, J. (2006). "The Next Innovation Revolution" pp. 123–144, in P. E. Auerswald & I. Z. Quadir (Eds.), *Innovations: Technology, Governance, Globalization.* Cambridge, MA: MIT Press.

Weiss, L. (2014). "US Technology Procurement in the National Security Innovation System" Chapter 13, pp. 259–285, in V. Lember, R. Kattel & T. Kalvet (Eds.), *Public Procurement, Innovation and Policy: International Perspectives.* New York: Springer.

Wessner, C. W. (Ed.) (1999). *The Small Business Innovation Research Program.* Washington, DC: National Academies Press. https://doi.org/10.17226/9701.

Wessner, C. W. (Ed.) (2008). *An Assessment of the SBIR Program.* Washington, DC: National Academies Press.

Wiggins, J. & D. V. Gibson (2003). "Overview of US Incubators and the Case of the Austin Technology Incubator," *International Journal of Entrepreneurship & Innovation Management,* 3(3), 56–66.

Wooten, M. (2015). "Organizational Fields" in *International Encyclopedia of the Social and Behavioral Sciences,* 2nd Edition, Amsterdam: Elsevier.

4   Case Studies
Austin, Texas, USA, and Tsuruoka, Yamagata, Japan

Boston R128 and Silicon Valley are perhaps the most well-recognized examples of successful regional research and development (R&D)-based innovation economies in the world. While there are clearly additional examples of successful regional technology-based growth economies, it has proved a difficult objective for many regions in the United States and worldwide (Kenney, 2000). In this chapter, we clarify what we consider important and generalizable conditions of successful endogenous tech-based economic growth through a comparative analysis of two city-regions in significantly different national contexts: Austin, Texas, USA, and Tsuruoka, Yamagata, Japan. In addition to significant differences in the cultures and institutions of these two city regions, we highlight important similarities in terms of how they successfully achieved tech-based economic growth.

The case of Austin describes how, in the mid-1980s, a university town and Texas capital city of about 431,000 began its trajectory to become a world-recognized R&D and innovation center that continues to grow in national and international significance as a thriving Technopolis.[1] The Tsuruoka's case focuses on how a city with a population of 140,000 and facing economic decline in the 1990s achieved a successful biotech IPO in a remarkably short period of time, which launched successful biotech industry regionwide. This "win" was locally motivated and funded, while other Japanese cities receiving financial support from the central government were not able to realize such success.[2]

Important components of institutional theory underpin our research methodology and discussion of Austin and Tsuruoka. First, social and political context are critical in building both "New Capital I" and "New Small i" institutions to support regional entrepreneurial activity and tech-based growth. Second, "robust actors" play a vital role in establishing regional "New Small i" institutions to support new technology firms and initiatives. Third, such actions are path-dependent in that contemporary success is inextricably linked to preexisting events and activities.

The cases of Austin and Tsuruoka both highlight catalytic or "trigger" events that initiated the building of "New Small i" institutions which provoked endogenous tech-based economic growth. In accordance with institutional

DOI: 10.4324/9781003488149-5

theory, we emphasize *how things happened* in addition to *what happened*. We show how "robust actors," bridging and spanning institutional boundaries, created critical support systems for realizing successful Technology Venturing. We also emphasize the interdependence of factors operating at multiple levels of analysis—regulative, normative, and cultural-cognitive—to build a supportive environment for entrepreneurs launching tech-based start-ups. We acknowledge some important distinctions between our two regions of study. Austin's case takes a broad perspective to describe a widespread regional transformation toward a globally competitive high-tech economy. Tsuruoka's case focuses on the establishment of an entrepreneurial university R&D center and an incubator supporting the launch of a tech-based startup and a regionally based biotech industry. While we note these differences, we also highlight similar characteristics and strategies of both regions such as building critically important "New Small i" institutions, having and sustaining a unifying vision, and the important role of "robust actors." Our objective is to provide useful and generalizable lessons at the company and incubator levels of development as well as at the regional level of analysis.

1   The Case of Austin, Texas

Our exploration of Austin's tech-based growth, focuses on the evolution of institutional processes in economic development, including how exogenous factors influenced institutional evolution toward endogenous innovation, how and why "Small i" institutions were formed and changed over time, and the role of "robust actors" in initiating and shaping relationships within and across Austin's public and private sectors. A fundamental premise of the institutional perspective of regional development is the importance of local context and history. Austin's historic identity and culture was importantly defined by being designated the capital of Texas in 1846 and as the location for the flagship campus of the University of Texas at Austin (UT Austin) in 1883.[3]

Austin provides an excellent test case for exploring the importance of local institutional processes in building a technology-based economy, in part, because in the mid-1980s it was considered a "least likely" place for regionally based R&D technology development (Gibson & Rogers, 1994). The city, of about 431,000 people exhibited low dynamism in its private sector and local economic development activity (Gibson and Oden, 2019). Austin's tech-based economy had benefitted from several noteworthy recruitment successes in the 1960s and 1970s including Xerox, Texas Instruments, Motorola, AMD, and Compaq-Tandem. In 1966, the Chamber of Commerce promoting Austin's and Texas' business-friendly environment (e.g., low taxes, non-union workforce, low start-up and operating costs) successfully recruited IBM to Austin to manufacture the Selectric typewriter. In terms of start-up activity, the main stand-out was Tracor, Inc., that in 1954 was spun out of UT Austin's Balcones Research Park by four university research scientists who successfully grew the company to become Austin's first <u>Fortune 500</u> company. However, into the mid-1980s, Austin's economy and identity was dominated by state government and The University of Texas. Importantly, the central Texas city also had a growing reputation as a center for creative talent (especially music and film) where young men and women wanted to live, despite the city's sparse job opportunities and career options. However, few, if any, local and national government, and business leaders saw Austin as having the potential to become a Technopolis or a major international research, innovation, and technology hub (Gibson & Rogers, 1994; Gibson & Oden, 2019).

Research articles, books, and the popular press have provided a range of explanations for Austin's rapid technology growth success, centering on the key role of UT Austin with 45,000 students and the high numbers of graduates in computer science (CS) and electrical engineering (EE). Others link the region's growth success to its high quality of life as exhibited in the natural assets of pristine lakes and tree-covered hills, an abundance of hike and bike trails (some located in the center of the city parallel to the Colorado River), tree covered parks and spring-fed pools, miles of running trails and a broad range of entertainment and recreational activities. Also noted as important is the cities relatively low cost of living (especially in the 1980s/1990s), and a growing reputation as a center of music and film creativity in attracting and building "the creative class" (Florida, 2002). In short, Austin was seen as a desirable place to live, get an advanced degree, raise a family, and perhaps start a company.

For the purposes of our case analysis, as we describe significant events and activities that contributed to Austin's technology-based growth success, our discussion centers on the formation of "New Small i" institutions, which we consider key to Austin's transformation in the late 1980s and 1990s as we focus on the community-based activities and actions taken by key "robust actors" who drove three important region-changing accomplishments:

1 Recruiting to Austin the Microelectronics and Computer Technology Corporation (MCC), the nation's first for profit industry-based technology R&D research consortium
2 Recruiting US and international technology companies to expand in and locate in the Austin region
3 Fostering and growing Austin's entrepreneurial and technology venturing economy by establishing "New Small i" institutions

1.1   A Transformational Event: Winning a National Competition for MCC

In 1982, Texas Governor Mark White was alerted that a major national competition was underway to select the location for the nation's first for-profit R&D consortium that was to propel US technology innovation and importantly to counter stiff Japanese technology competition. The MCC was financed by and otherwise supported by some of the country's leading technology firms including Advanced Micro Devices, Motorola, Boeing, National

Semiconductor Corporation, 3M (Minnesota Mining & Manufacturing), RCA (Radio Corporation of America)/General Electric, CDC (Control Data Corporation), Honeywell Corporation, DEC (Digital Equipment Corporation), Hughes Corporation, and Hewlett-Packard. Fifty-six cities in 27 states initially competed to win the competition—a list which the MCC site selection committee narrowed to four finalists: Raleigh-Durham, North Carolina; Atlanta, Georgia; San Diego, California; and Austin, Texas. MCC's final site selection decision focused on the following criteria (Gibson & Rogers, 1994):

1 Access to a local university with the resources and vision to be a national and world leader in research and education in electrical engineering (EE) and computer science (CS)
2 Regional high quality of life including recreational and cultural amenities, high-level primary and secondary education, and affordable housing
3 Good airline connections to the cities of MCC member company headquarters (Austin's relatively small regional airport was considered a significant weakness, but the use of corporate jets was seen as a partial solution to this challenge)
4 State and local government support for MCC
5 Low overall cost of launching and operating MCC at the proposed site

In the final weeks of the competition, of the four final candidates, Austin was ranked last by the MCC site selection committee, so national public and private leaders and economic development experts were stunned when the Capital City of Texas was announced the winner. Gibson and Rogers (1994) contend that Austin won because, in addition to meeting essential requirements like having a major research university with a vision to grow in stature, the Texas recruitment team was more competent in (1) understanding what the MCC site selection committee wanted to see in the winning bid and (2) successfully working to fulfill MCC's expectations through extensive and effective public/private information gathering and collaboration at national, state, and regional levels. Governor White formed a task force composed of seven business and banking leaders from Austin and Dallas; five government leaders including the governor and his executive assistant Pike Powers; and leaders from the University of Texas and Texas A&M University Systems. At the city level, an Austin task force included seven prominent business leaders as well as three members from the governor's task force again including Pike Powers and representatives from UT Austin and Texas A&M University.

As participants coming from the state's public and private sectors, the Texas team brought together a broad range of professional accomplishment and experience as well as an expanded network of personal relationships. Gibson and Rogers (1994) emphasize the importance of these "robust actors" who successfully networked across the region's business, government, and academic sectors to win the MCC competition. We focus our discussion at the individual level of analysis as represented by Pike Powers, a key member of both the Texas and Austin teams, who exemplified the personal and professional skills needed to build the alliances and partnerships, at normative and cultural-cognitive levels of analysis, to achieve the desired goals. As remembered by Ray Perryman (2021):

> As a successful lawyer living in Austin, Pike Powers spearheaded the successful effort to attract MCC. Texas normally did not compete for such things. Rich natural resource endowments had long insulated the state from the vicissitudes confronting other economic growth models. The battle to bring this desperately needed diversification was importantly one of convincing folks within Texas as well as the MCC site-selection committees. Pike possessed the skills of an extraordinary "deal-making" attorney, remarkable political acumen, an ability to forge consensus among disparate groups, an intellect to visualize a better future, and an uncanny knack for show-stopping presentations.
>
> Pike experienced personal and professional challenges that would have broken lesser souls, but never once lost his optimism or passion. Pike steered Austin's proposal for MCC through a legislative minefield. Later, he worked with others on the Texas Technology Initiative, which helped Texas evolve as emphasis shifted from chips and hardware to software, gaming, biosciences, materials science, and nanotechnology. Even as his health deteriorated, his enthusiasm endured. He was always focused forward. Texas's technology footprint constantly expands, but the fingerprints inevitably include those of Pike Powers. The state will no doubt persist in its quest for global technology supremacy. No matter the height reached, however, it will always stand on the shoulders of and rest in the shadow of this genuine Texas giant whose spirit and legacy will never diminish.

Building the needed cross-institutional alliances was challenging at times, even with the full support of the Texas governor, the Texas team members, and their colleagues. For example, securing committed support from UT Austin to win the bid for MCC was not the "slam dunk" one might expect. The MCC opportunity was not brought to UT President Peter Flawn by his own trusted advisors, and he was dubious of having "his" state-supported university partnering with this pathbreaking private-sector R&D consortium. However, Gerry Fonken, UT's vice president for research and academic affairs along with Professor Herbert Woodson of UT's department of EE, and Ben Streetman, a newly recruited and highly regarded EE professor, believed MCC would fit nicely into the department's strategic plan to achieve world-class excellence in microelectronics and computer engineering.

> It's difficult to imagine…how much of a challenge it was in 1983 for people to accept the idea for a major collaboration like MCC. There was the fear of antitrust and the framework for facilitating collaboration….

the real technology to come out of MCC was the technology of partnering; however, nobody realized just how difficult that was going to be (paraphrasing comments of Bob Price who chaired the steering committee and interim board of directors' meetings that gave birth to MCC (Gibson and Rogers, 1994: p. 257).

Often in community development projects, some of the less well-known and less-celebrated actors are, in fact, key to achieving success. In the Austin case of MCC's recruitment, Cliff Drummond, the associate director of UT's Center for Energy Studies, played a critical bridge-building role between academic, business, and government leaders. While not a high-level University of Texas official, Drummond was a close colleague to Professor Woodson and proved to be a key link between (1) the main players on the governor's and Austin task forces and (2) UT Austin. Drummond had state-wide political contacts and instincts, having run the Austin office of US Congressman Jake Pickle. He also had another important value to the MCC effort, as stated by Pike Powers: "He was relatively invisible and expendable if something went wrong.... A main reason I give Drummond so much credit is that he was a man without a title" (Gibson & Rogers, 1994, p. 64).

As an important part of Texas/Austin's winning bid for MCC, UT Austin agreed to triple the size of its microelectronics research program by establishing 30 new endowed professorships in electrical engineering (EE) and computer science (CS). Usually such a strategic outlay of resources would involve years of planning and involve faculty members and administrators as well as complicated budget maneuvering. But in Spring 1983, the university had two weeks. In short, all the usual planning procedures were largely ignored, no faculty committees, no detailed budget planning (Gibson & Rogers, 1994, p. 159). Yet they succeeded in meeting this milestone and indeed exceeding their initial expectations[4].

In summary, Austin's pivot toward an innovation economy was catalyzed by key "robust actors" who voluntarily, and largely outside of their normal workday responsibilities, engaged in cross-sector public-private networking and relationship-building in pursuit of a common economic development vision and strategy for the Austin region. As remembered by Pike Powers:

I still get kind of a special tingle about the people that were involved. Nobody ever said "No." Nobody ever complained. Everybody just did what they were supposed to do, and more. There was a sense that we were on a special mission. The MCC competition was more important than anything most people had worked on before. We couldn't flub it... People just rose to the occasion... and did more than they probably thought they were capable of doing and they exceeded their own capacity. You have an incredibly good performance by human beings who are otherwise very flawed and very normal and very ordinary.
(Pike Powers Interview, March 27, 1986: Gibson & Rogers, 1994, p. 134)

In Storper's words (2015, p. 94), "only accidents that sow seeds on fertile ground live to see the future." The Austin case illustrates how MCC's recruitment educated and positioned regional "robust actors" to successfully exploit future economic development opportunities. Indeed, an important follow-on benefit from Austin winning the MCC included winning the 1988 national competition for SEMATECH—a groundbreaking government and private-sector-funded US R&D consortium which focused on semiconductor research. But perhaps most importantly, significant personal connections and relationships were strengthened among regional leaders across business, academic, and government sectors to collectively envision Austin's regional transformation to become a globally competitive Technopolis.

1.2   Technology Firm Recruitment

In 1986, Austin was hard hit by financial crises in both real estate and the savings and loan industries. An associated overall economic downturn resulted in "see through" (vacant) buildings and high numbers of bankruptcies. In 1987, the managing director of Standard & Poor's informed state leadership that if Texas did not diversify its economy, the state would see its bond rating lowered (Epstein, 2019). To help address these concerns, the Austin Chamber of Commerce hired Glenn West—the president and CEO of the Macon Georgia Chamber of Commerce—to head Austin's chamber.

One of West's first jobs was to lead the effort to win the national competition for SEMATECH. As stated by Austin's Mayor Lee Cooke in 1988, "A lot of selfless people did what was needed to recruit SEMATECH and to make Austin a better place for people they had never met and would never know" (Cooke, 2019). West considered the support and involvement of UT Austin as crucial to successfully recruiting SEMATECH, so he called university president Bill Cunningham to calendar an upcoming site selection visit. After talking for about 15 minutes, Cunningham said, "This is too important. How about my spending the day with you?" As West observed, "Everyone I called—from businesses to the city, and the university—gave their time and commitment to the recruitment effort" (West, 2016).

As Austin continued to benefit from recruitment efforts, national observers began to see the Capital City as an important emerging technology region with growing R&D capabilities. Austin's local development coalition aggressively leveraged these perceptions to accelerate and deepen their efforts to attract technology-based firms to the Austin region. These activities focused on California, and about two times a year, the Chamber led Austin business and civic leaders on company recruitment visits to Silicon Valley. As West remembered, "since Austin had successfully recruited MCC, 3M Research, and SEMATECH, we usually received a warm reception. We talked about Austin's low cost of living, the excellence of The University of Texas at Austin, and the region's high quality of life" (West, 2016). Many of these targeted recruitment efforts were successful in securing branch plant expansions including Applied Materials in 1989, Hewlett-Packard in 1991, Apple and Cisco in 1992, Samsung and Silicon Labs in 1996, and many other others.

The critical roles of specialization, agglomeration, and localized increasing returns in explaining rapid growth are well understood (Marshall, 1986; Sivianidou & Polenske, 1988). In this context, the rapid expansion of Austin's major technology firms signaled a widening and deepening of industrial agglomeration processes and branch plants expanded their local operations into research and corporate product development activities (Gibson & Oden, 2019). For example, although IBM chose Austin for a manufacturing facility in 1966—by 1986 the company had expanded its Austin-based R&D operations to become one of the company's major international research centers.

One key event in the region's economic turnaround was the recruitment of Applied Materials in 1989. Austin Mayor Lee Cooke worked with the city mayor of a neighboring county to get a seven-year tax abatement by showing the considerable tax benefits to the local school district. Cooke provided the data illustrating that one year of Applied Materials taxes would equal all the taxes the Independent School District had previously collected on the vacant rural land. Many semiconductor industry suppliers and customers followed Applied Materials, to be located near the Austin facility, which also strengthened regional job mobility opportunities. By the early 1990s, the Austin region's dominant industry was semiconductor design and manufacturing including Samsung, Motorola, AMD, and several smaller chip fabrication facilities (Ladendorf, 1997). It is important to note that these operations were much more than just a cluster of advanced manufacturing plants. For example, Motorola's Oak Hill Facility became world headquarters for their communications and advanced consumer technologies, microcontroller technology, and microprocessor and memory technology groups (Gibson & Oden, 2015). By the mid-1990s, these design and fabrication establishments were linked to local R&D centers and specialized equipment suppliers including Applied Materials, Lam Research, and Tokyo Electron (Oden & Yilmaz, 2005).

As national corporations located and expanded in Austin, important institutional elements and relationships emerged, reshaping the networks of local economic development institutions, as well as the direction of Austin's economic growth. At the normative and cognitive levels of analysis, this evolution included a move toward a decidedly pro-development stance of business and civic leaders; an expansion of business, civic, and university collaboration around industrial development; and the targeting of sectors seen as compatible with the region's unique assets, as well as its business and cultural preferences. Linkages between corporate branch plants and parent corporations not only brought talent and knowledge of microelectronics and computing product markets to the Austin region they also facilitated personal connections between local civic and university leaders with managers of high-growth firms based in other leading US technology regions (Gibson & Oden, 2019). However, through the 1980s, Austin's local growth coalition was only weakly attentive to indigenous small firm growth or fostering technology-based startups. As noted by Glenn West, "During my tenure as President of Austin's Chamber (1987–2003) our predominant focus was on recruiting company expansions from Silicon Valley" (Interview, March 16, 2016).

1.2.1   Important Beginnings of Austin's Entrepreneurial Tech-Based Growth

The role of large firms as powerful incubators of entrepreneurial startups is well documented (Avnimelech & Feldman, 2010; Klepper, 2010; Schoar, 2010). Three pioneering entrepreneurial startup successes that contributed importantly to Austin's tech-based growth were the founding of Tracor, Inc. in 1955, National Instruments in 1976, and PC's Limited in 1984 (now DELL Technologies Inc.). All three of these tech-based startups were directly linked to UT Austin, and all three can be identified as high-innovation companies (Kanter, 1985), incubator organizations (Cooper, 1985), or "anchor tenants" (Storper, 2013). These founding success stories accelerated national recruitment of talent to Austin and provided powerful positive examples and role models for local entrepreneurs and investors.

Frank McBee earned a bachelor and master's degree in mechanical engineering from UT Austin. In 1950, he became the supervisor of UT Austin's Defense Research Laboratory (now called the Applied Research Laboratories) at the University's Balcones Research Park. In 1955, he was recruited by Richard Lane along with two other UT physicists to form Associated Consultants and Engineers, Inc. focusing their research on acoustic noise reduction technology. In 1957, they founded Texas Research Associates (TRA) which merged with Textran in 1962 to form Tracor, Inc. becoming Austin's first home-grown Fortune 500 company. By 1985, at least 16 companies had spun out of Tracor, and several of these companies' created spinouts of their own (Smilor et al., 1989).

In the early 1970s, James Truchard, Jeff Kodosky, and Bill Nowlin were working at UT Austin's Applied Research Laboratories conducting research for the US Navy. Frustrated with inefficient data collection methods that were available they developed innovative technology in Truchard's home garage and founded National Instruments (NI) in 1976. In 1983, NI developed its first General Purpose Interface Bus to connect instruments to IBM personal computers (PCs). With the arrival of Apple's Macintosh computer, NI researcher's collaborated with UT Austin students to identify ways to exploit this new interface. In 1986, NI presented LabVIEW graphical development platform for the Macintosh computer. When the company went public in 1995, over 300 current and former employees benefitted from owning NI stock.

In 1983, Michael Dell began his undergraduate studies at UT Austin and—drawing on his entrepreneurial interest in the emerging personal computer industry—built and sold upgraded PCs and add-on components to his fellow students. In his second year at UT, at age 19, he dropped out of school and with $1,000 in startup capital founded PC's Limited, selling custom-built computers directly to end users. Important local civic leaders saw the potential of Dell and PC's Limited, and they mentored the young entrepreneur and invested in his company (Dell & Fredman, 1999; Dell & Kaplan, 2021). Dell Computer Corporation went public in 1988, and the company's stock rapidly increased in value. Early Dell employees and investors became "Dellionaires" and many participated in and contributed to Austin's entrepreneur economy and civic activities. Dell Technologies Inc. (formerly and Dell Computer Corporation) has had, and continues to have, massive positive impacts on the Austin/Round Rock city regions including the attraction and retention of national and international talent, funding contributions to the University of Texas at Austin and Dell Medical School, and additional corporate giving and regional philanthropy including the Michael and Susan Dell Foundation.

During the 1980s, other technology company startups and spinouts were happening in the Austin region, and one of the most prominent examples of this entrepreneurial activity was Tivoli, which was launched by three Austin-based IBM engineers in 1989. Overtime Tivoli employees founded more than 30 Austin-based spinouts and startups (Echeverri-Caroll et al., 2018). With Austin's growing cluster of technology firms "New Small i" institutional support, a critical foundation for entrepreneurial spinoffs and startups, was starting to take hold in the Austin region.

1.3   *Innovation, Creativity and Capital (IC²) Institute*

While recruiting MCC and technology companies was key to Austin's regional tech-based economic development, in the mid-1980s the region lacked widespread entrepreneurial activity and startup culture. Austin's Greater Chamber of Commerce did not actively support business entrepreneurship and neither did UT-Austin. However, the seeds of change were laid in 1966 when the University recruited George Kozmetsky to be Dean of the college and graduate school of business. With a PhD in commercial science from Harvard University and teaching experience at Carnegie Mellon University and later co-founding Teledyne Technologies Inc. in California in 1960, Kozmetsky was an inspired hire (Jones, 2018).[5] In 1977, during his tenure as Dean, Kozmetsky—working with colleagues and friends from UT Austin and nationally—founded the IC² (Innovation, Creativity and Capital) Institute at UT Austin. Kozmetsky differentiated his Institute as a "think and do tank"—aiming to pursue research and catalyze regional technology-based growth through:

- Dynamic small business and entrepreneurship programs
- Cultural, ethical, and institutional studies

- Policy issues and analysis programs
- Private enterprise education programs

After retiring as Dean in 1983, Kozmetsky became full-time director of IC² Institute where he emphasized the importance of networking and collaboration across government, academic, and industry sectors as a key regional dynamic for new venture creation. In "Breaking the Mold: Reinventing Business Through Community Collaboration," a paper delivered at the MIT Enterprise Forum, Kozmetsky (1993) stated:

> The solutions to many critical issues and problems now demand an integrated, holistic and flexible approach that blends technology, management, and scientific, socio-economic, cultural and political ramifications in an atmosphere of profound change and extreme time compression.

Under Kozmetsky's leadership, the IC² Institute built a prestigious Fellows Program of national and international leaders from academia, government, and business. Kozmetsky had a gift for bringing diverse talent together, and the Institute staff and Fellows published books, monographs, and articles on a broad range of topics—many focusing on technology-based regional development. As a "Think and Do" tank, the Institute was a key catalyst in the launch and management of three "Small i" institutions that contributed support to Austin's early entrepreneurial development and growth:

1 *The Austin Technology Incubator (ATI):* to educate UT-Austin and regional entrepreneurs how best to incubate and grow technology startups.
2 *The Texas Capital Network (TCN):* to educate investors on high-tech startup funding and growth, as well as facilitating the introduction of investors and entrepreneurs.
3 *The Austin Software Council (ASC):* to provide Austin area entrepreneurs with networking and mentoring support.

While each of these entities became a model for entrepreneurial support activities nationally and internationally, it is noteworthy that Kozmetsky and his colleagues launched these "Small i" institutions while these concepts were unproven in their form and function Perhaps most importantly, these activities facilitated interaction and cooperation among "robust actors" in government, academia, and industry leading to "Small i" institutional development critical to building Austin's technology-based entrepreneurial economy.

1.3.1   *The (Austin Technology Incubator (ATI)*

In 1984, shortly after Austin won MCC, a regional study by SRI International concluded that Austin's future economic development would be hindered by a lack of entrepreneurship and indigenous technology-based growth. Glenn West, President of Austin's Chamber of Commerce, accepted this conclusion as stated below:

> On my first day at work, I met George [Kozmetsky] as we were in a meeting at the chamber about recruiting SEMATECH to Austin. After the meeting, George and I met for an hour or so. Having seen a technology incubator started at Georgia Tech, I asked about not having one in Austin and George responded, "So let's start one. You get the chamber to put some money in and we will get the city and county to do the same." It took a while, but eventually ATI (The Austin Technology Incubator) became a reality. George had been thinking about it for some time, but this was our first conversation on the topic. In that first meeting George also told me we should work to make Austin a "Technopolis" and I give him credit for much of the strategic thinking that made Austin the technology and innovation center it is today.
>
> (West, 2019)

The ATI was launched near the geographical location of Austin's emerging software cluster, in 4,000 square feet of "borrowed" office space using university storage and "difficult to sell and damaged" furniture donated by Austin retail stores. As a successful California-based entrepreneur, Kozmetsky could have simply underwritten the startup expenses of ATI; however, he wanted to secure active buy-in and commitment from key public and private stakeholders—and he also wanted to jump-start a regional entrepreneurial culture which he saw as being critical to launching and sustaining the management and operation of ATI. Accordingly, Kozmetsky, ATI's founding director Laura Kilcrease, and chamber and city collaborators worked to secure modest three-year funding for ATI: $50,000/year from the City of Austin; $25,000/year from the Greater Austin Chamber of Commerce (GACC); a one-time donation of $70,000 from Travis County, and $50,000 from a private donor. Administrators and faculty at UT Austin were not entirely comfortable with a state-supported educational institution serving as host for a business incubator in which select private member companies would receive benefits and could profit financially, even if the incubator itself was nonprofit. UT support increased when the concept of ATI was presented by Kozmetsky and Kilcrease as a technology venturing "laboratory" for the education of students and professors—much like a chemistry or physics lab. Classes on technology marketing, venture finance, management, and entrepreneurship were taught at ATI, while student interns worked with ATI's startup companies.

Training was also offered to the broader Austin community on business plan development, venture finance, and technology marketing. An important and critical success factor for ATI was launching a "know-how network" composed of regionally based lawyers, accountants, management consultants, and business angels who volunteered time to mentor ATI companies and whose main financial return on investment was in helping entrepreneurs who might one day develop into paying clients. From its inception, ATI pursued the dual purpose of being (1) an education and research laboratory for entrepreneurship and technology venturing, and (2) a regional catalyst to help entrepreneurs launch startups that would contribute to Austin's economic development. For example, ATI's Student Entrepreneur Acceleration and Launch (SEAL) program identified promising student entrepreneurial teams from across UT Austin colleges and departments and engaged them in an intensive 12-week summer education program, involving community and industry mentors and subject matter experts, to help bring the team members to a "go" or "no-go" decision. SEAL program instructors emphasized that a "no-go" decision was as important and respected as a "go" decision, on the theory that it is better to "fail quickly" and move on to another entrepreneurial project, rather than invest extended time and resources in a flawed business proposition. This "freedom to fail" helped invest SEAL students with an entrepreneurial mindset that was independent from the success or failure of a single business concept. Over a period of six years, about one third of the SEAL companies failed, another third bootstrapped successfully, and the remaining third collectively raised about $12 million in private capital markets.

As depicted by Figure 4.1, as Austin's regional innovation and entrepreneurial support systems grew and matured, so did ATI. From 1989 to 2015, ATI incubation activities migrated across four Intellectual Property (IP)-based technology verticals: Information Technology (IT), clean energy, wireless, and biosciences. ATI provided its portfolio of companies with access to industry-specific management expertise, investor networks, and talent. It is important to note that each of these industry verticals had important formal and informal links to UT Austin research and education as well as to city and chamber of commerce economic development objectives. As of 2024, ATI at UT Austin is focused on "deep tech" or technology that is based on tangible engineering innovation, scientific advances, and discoveries.

In summary, ATI has been central to assisting regional entrepreneurs build successful business teams to support technology ventures and to better access angel, Venture Capital, and state funding; mentoring students from across campus; working with the city, chamber, and regional business community to help strengthen emerging technology sectors, and in graduating potential high-growth ventures into the Austin community. With financial and other support from the University of Texas, the City of Austin, and local business professionals, ATI has the distinction of being the longest active technology incubator in the nation and has mentored more than 500 companies that have realized more than 10 IPOs, more than 50 mergers or acquisitions, raised more than $2 billion in venture capital funds, and provided a regional economic impact of more than $3 billion.[6] Moreover, as ATI was an important catalyst in the Austin region.it has been a model for successful business incubation in other US and international regions. In 2016, IC^2 research identified

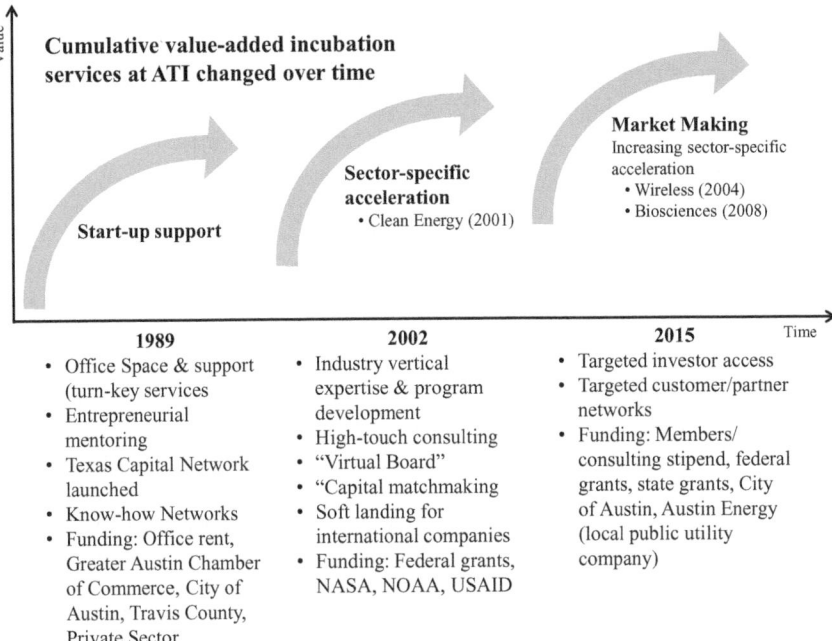

Cumulative value-added incubation services at ATI changed over time

Market Making
Increasing sector-specific acceleration
• Wireless (2004)
• Biosciences (2008)

Sector-specific acceleration
• Clean Energy (2001)

Start-up support

1989	2002	2015
• Office Space & support (turn-key services • Entrepreneurial mentoring • Texas Capital Network launched • Know-how Networks • Funding: Office rent, Greater Austin Chamber of Commerce, City of Austin, Travis County, Private Sector	• Industry vertical expertise & program development • High-touch consulting • "Virtual Board" • "Capital matchmaking • Soft landing for international companies • Funding: Federal grants, NASA, NOAA, USAID	• Targeted investor access • Targeted customer/partner networks • Funding: Members/consulting stipend, federal grants, state grants, City of Austin, Austin Energy (local public utility company)

Figure 4.1 ATI Evolved as Did Austin's Technology Venturing Ecosystem

Source: Authors

39 profit and nonprofit business incubators, accelerators, and co-working spaces in the Austin area.[7] Many of these entities are civic and culturally oriented activities in addition to technology-focused ventures, and their existence reflects a broad-based regional support for entrepreneurial activity as an important component of the Austin Model.

1.3.2   *The Capital Network (TCN)*

A lack of venture or angel capital in the Austin region in 1989 was a distinct challenge for the successful operation of ATI and, more generally, the region-wide growth of entrepreneurial ventures. Recognizing this need, Kozmetsky, Kilcrease, and their colleagues traveled the state to meet and talk with wealthy Texans (who were experienced in making real estate and energy investments) to better understand the risk profiles of technology-based ventures. As Meg Wilson (2016), who was working with the Texas governor's office at the time, remembered:

> As we traveled the state, we met with chamber of commerce groups, rotary groups, business clubs, women's clubs, local leadership groups, etc. Our message was simple: many wealthy Texans knew how to

invest in real estate and oil and gas, but both sectors have a very short risk profile as they tend to be up or down within a year. Technology often has a risk profile of 5 to10 years, or more for biotechnology. We were suggesting that they start investing in economic diversification by putting a fiscally responsible portion of their investments into technology.

Texas Capital Network (TCN) participants agreed to review business plans in specific technology sectors and, if they so desired, provide seed funding to an entrepreneurial venture. TCN, which was based at ATI, was renamed The Capital Network (TCN) as it grew to be the largest angel fund in the Southwest, facilitating more than $150 million in total investments for about 2,000 registered entrepreneurs. TCN hosted annual venture capital conferences which attracted upward of 300–500 investors and entrepreneurs who came from across the state and nation to hear venture pitches from Texas startups. From 1989 into the 1990s, TCN provided crucial training, visibility, seed capital, and mentoring to Austin's technology startups and was instrumental in launching a regional Angel Fund with the support of the Austin Chamber of Commerce and in attracting additional private venture capital firms to open offices in Austin. The relatively short lifespan of the TCN as an organization is, in itself, perhaps an important facet of the successful regional implementation of "Small i" institutions, inasmuch as they may serve a specific mentoring niche that shifts as community entrepreneurship evolves and new actors emerge.

1.3.3   The Austin Technology Council (ATC)

In 1991, the Austin Entrepreneur's Council (AEC) was formed by IC^2 Institute to help network the region's entrepreneurs, to arrange educational and speaker venues, and to provide mentoring for Austin's emerging entrepreneurial community. After a few months of operation and at the suggestion of UT Austin computer science professors and regional software industry leaders, Kozmetsky was encouraged to focus activities and support on the growing regional software industry. In 1992, repurposing the AEC, the Austin Software Council (ASC) was launched at a press conference that included Austin's mayor and Chamber of Commerce officials; UT professors and staff; industry representatives from MCC, IBM, and other regionally based companies as well as startup software businesses. Standing committees held monthly Tiger Workshops on select topics of interest, and larger conferences were held on emerging areas of importance. Dinner meetings were held at MCC that featured keynote speakers for people to discuss software research, marketing, finance, and start-ups. In 1993, IC^2 Institute and the Greater Austin Chamber of Commerce published *The Greater Austin Software Industry Report*, which described Austin's software industry growth timeline, research funding, and areas of industry expertise.

By the late 1990s, other regional technology sectors were gaining strength, and in 2000, the ASC was renamed the Austin Technology Council (ATC) to address these broader needs, as the organization became an advocate for Central Texas's technology and life science industries. This type of organizational shift illustrates, again, the important needed agility of "Small i" institution to be able to evolve to meet specific local needs. In 2024, ATC works to increase access to technology talent, seed and venture capital, market visibility, and support for emerging technology sectors. ATC shares the relevant insights of local, state, and national leaders to optimize collaboration and reduce gaps between private industry and public investment to foster a more competitive and sustainable regional economy through community connections and activities.

In summary, in the early 1990s, ATI, TCN, and ASC were innovative "Small i" foundational programs that helped catalyze and build public-private networks to support regional entrepreneurs in business plan development, deal structuring and managing investment processes. It is perhaps worthwhile to note that while ATI was created as a part of the IC^2 Institute and UT Austin, both the TCN and the ATC operated outside the auspices of the University's oversight. Kozmetsky's vision for regional innovation was one that—rather than control—sought to educate, inspire, and enable regional talent in entrepreneurial pursuits. As described above, these three "Small i" institutions facilitated knowledge spillovers, connectivity, and mentoring vital to normative and cultural-cognitive change important to the growth and sustainability of Austin's entrepreneurial innovation ecosystem (Figure 4.2).

1.4   Austin's Cultural Context

While at times hard to define, it is well recognized that regional culture can have strong positive or perhaps negative impact on developing and sustaining entrepreneurial ecosystems including the attraction and retention of talent (Florida, 2002). Sometimes referred to as the "magic" or "spirit" of a place, it is no less real for remaining undefined.[8] Storper (2013) mentioned the importance of the Bay Area's counterculture in providing a supportive environment for fostering creativity and enabling "robust actors" and innovators to pursue new ways of doing things. Austin, Texas, is known for its counterculture "Keep Austin Weird" vibe, especially in the creative industries. The city carries considerable gravitas to its claim as "The Live Music Capital of the World" as exemplified by the award-winning and long-running *Austin City Limits* public broadcast TV production and its annual Fall music festival, as well as the annual South by Southwest (SXSW) music, film, and digital two-week conference and festival.[9] Despite its rapid growth and escalating cost of living, Austin has been able to retain important aspects of its "counterculture" and friendly "small town" feeling as new arrivals get involved with and participate in a broad range of entrepreneurial, nonprofit, entertainment,

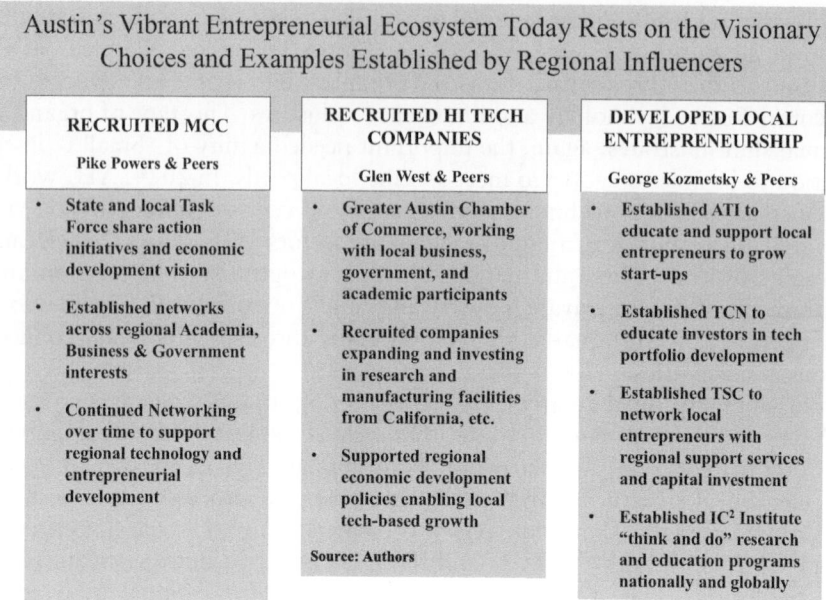

Austin's Vibrant Entrepreneurial Ecosystem Today Rests on the Visionary Choices and Examples Established by Regional Influencers

RECRUITED MCC Pike Powers & Peers	**RECRUITED HI TECH COMPANIES** Glen West & Peers	**DEVELOPED LOCAL ENTREPRENEURSHIP** George Kozmetsky & Peers
• State and local Task Force share action initiatives and economic development vision • Established networks across regional Academia, Business & Government interests • Continued Networking over time to support regional technology and entrepreneurial development	• Greater Austin Chamber of Commerce, working with local business, government, and academic participants • Recruited companies expanding and investing in research and manufacturing facilities from California, etc. • Supported regional economic development policies enabling local tech-based growth Source: Authors	• Established ATI to educate and support local entrepreneurs to grow start-ups • Established TCN to educate investors in tech portfolio development • Established TSC to network local entrepreneurs with regional support services and capital investment • Established IC² Institute "think and do" research and education programs nationally and globally

Figure 4.2 Foundational "Small i" Initiatives of "the Austin Model" for Tech-Based Development

Source: Authors

recreational, educational, and civic-oriented activities. Additionally, Austin provides an interesting state-wide contrast by being the lone "blueberry" (Democrat) region in the tomato soup of a big "red" (Republican) state.

2   The case of Tsuruoka, Yamagata, Japan

2.1   *A City Facing the Risk of Extinction*

Known as the castle town of Shonai fief in the Edo era and located in Yamagata Prefecture facing the Sea of Japan, Tsuruoka has served as the region's central municipality for nearly 400 years. Japan's regional economies had been sustained—from the recovery and high economic growing period after World War II to the bubble burst—through three pillars: (1) manufacturing plants established by big businesses, (2) public construction programs, and (3) subsidies to sustain rice farmers. The income from any one of these three components has historically been relatively low compared to earnings by metropolitan workers. To mitigate these challenges, many farmers operate a part-time farming household and working in local factories and public works projects during the off-farm season for rice cultivation. These activities help large segments of Japan's population gain slightly higher earnings than the national average income brought by the abovementioned three pillars. While the city of Tsuruoka was not designated as a candidate Technopolis under Japan's "Technopolis Policy" that was launched in the early 1980s, it nevertheless succeeded in inviting semiconductor manufacturing facilities to the region in the mid-1970s due, in part, to an influx of women to the workplace. It was believed woman's small and dexterous hands was a hiring advantage in many factory environments.[10] However, from 1985, this strong manufacturing presence declined due to high appreciation of the Yen that was forced by the Plaza Accord. The resulting bubble economy, which burst in the early 1990s, accelerated these declining trends toward a severe economic slump.

The effects of the bubble burst impacted every region of Japan and continues to be of high concern ten years later. A 2014 report projected that an astonishing number of 896 cities, towns, and villages (equal to 49.8% of Japanese municipalities) might be faced with extinction by 2040 if these regional economies were not successfully rejuvenated (Masuda, 2014). Like the most Japanese cities, Tsuruoka was also negatively impacted by the sudden drain of business establishments and decreasing employment exacerbated by the soaring Yen, rising labor costs, and a slump in domestic markets for the region's Integrated Circuit (IC) manufacturing as companies relocated to mainland China and ASEAN countries.[11] The city's population declined from 152K in 1986 to 142K in 2006, and the number of establishments with four or more employees fell from 533 to 346 during the same time. At the municipal level, a common response to a threat of urban extinction was to seek Central Government funds for public construction monies and agricultural subsidies. However, Y. Tomizuka, the visionary mayor of Tsuruoka City (who held office from 1991 to 2009) eschewed these traditional economic policies. Rather, he envisioned rejuvenating Tsuruoka's economy by recruiting needed talent, focusing on top researchers and students who were conducting advanced research at universities, especially in the field of life science. In 1996, Tomizuka set aside a special budget to invite a topnotch Japanese research university to open a life science department and research facility in Tsuruoka city.

Keio University, a premier private education and research institution, accepted Mayor Tomizuka's invitation largely due to his enthusiasm and vision, which was backed by concrete financial resources. Accordingly, in 2001, Keio University established the Institute for Advance Biosciences (IAB), in Tsuruoka City, including a graduate school program, as its first research institution outside its main campuses located in Tokyo. Mayor Tomizuka persuaded Yamagata Prefecture to contribute to both building costs and research funds, in addition to municipal funding which included salaries and other support for cutting-edge research activities at IAB.[12] It was a rare policy response for a Japanese city government to support such research expenses even after attracting a private university to the region.

Under the strong leadership of its founding director, Dr. M. Tomita, IAB pursued Mode Two-type transdisciplinary research activities (Gibbons et al., 1994). Tomita had studied at Carnegie Melon University (CMU) in Pittsburgh,

Pennsylvania, USA, where the entrepreneurial mission was strong, along with the traditional university missions of research and teaching. Tomita followed this model as he set to build IAB as an entrepreneurial university. Importantly, IAB was established as "a joint project between Yamagata Prefecture, Tsuruoka City, and Keio University" with the objective of rejuvenating the regional economy. This was an exceptional case in Japan, in the early 2000s, as IAB established itself as an entrepreneurial university pursuing regional economic growth through commercializing cutting-edge and breakthrough research results. According to Ishida (2014), IAB researchers and staff members appreciated Tomizuka's vision of securing a global reputation in systems biology, while working to rejuvenate Tsuruoka's economy based on commercializing IAB's research results, rather than depending on corporate factories and subsidiaries of the Central Government.

2.2   *Breakthrough Technological Invention*

The IAB's most focused research project was E-cell exploration which clarifies a cell's function through computer simulation. While intracellular metabolism analysis had become quite important in E-cell research, a technology impasse was inherent to gas chromatography's painstakingly slow analytical measures with low accuracy. Tomita recruited Dr. T. Soga, a talented specialist in developing analytical devices as an associate professor. Soga's industry-based R&D experience helped him develop the capillary electrophoresis-time-of-flight mass spectrometer (CE-TOFMS) analytical method at IAB, overcoming an important technology impasse through "Use-inspired basic research." This innovation utilizes CE as the breakthrough technology to separate metabolites effectively and accurately, so they can be identified through a TOFMS. This breakthrough technology revolutionized metabolite analysis allowing thousands of metabolites to be analyzed in a fraction of the time compared to existing gas chromatography/mass spectrometry (GC/MS) methods (Soga, 2004).

Keio University filed Soga's invention with the Japan Patent Office (JPO) in July 2001 and was awarded a patent in August 2002, an extraordinarily short timeframe for awarding a patent in Japan. However, in spite of being awarded patent protection, no Japanese company stepped forward to commercialize this breakthrough technology because, after genome decoding, proteome was then perceived as the main research field in biosciences. The Technology Licensing Organization (TLO) at Keio University actively sought candidate licensees without success, as companies failed to realize the commercial potential of this disruptive analytical method in the field of metabolome. Despite having a patented, transformative technology from a premier research university Keio University's TLO could not cross "the Valley of Death" and produce a commercially viable product with industry partners.

2.3   Supporting the University Tech-Based Startup

Technology Venturing was necessary to commercialize this breakthrough technology, however the project was initially without a business-oriented entrepreneur, which contributed to the delay in its commercialization. The inventor, Soga, then associate professor, had taken the position in order to pursue his research apart from industry's for-profit restraints, and he had no intention of launching a startup company. Importantly, Dr. Y. Otaki, President of Bio Frontier Partners Inc. (BFP), a venture capitalist specializing in life sciences, recognized the technology's disruptive potential, and in 2003, he launched Human Metabolome Technologies Inc. (HMT) to commercialize this breakthrough technology.[13]

Relying on Soga's cooperation and support, Otaki fulfilled the dual roles of entrepreneur and venture capitalist, becoming the first president of HMT, even as he provided funding through BFP. Venture capitalists usually take on a startup venture only after scrutinizing an entrepreneur's business plan. However, Otaki recognized the importance of the newly patented metabolome analytical technology in Japan's life science development. As a tech-based startup, HMT needed incubator services to reduce the high risks the company faced in Early-Stage Technology Development (ESTD); however, there was no such facility close to IAB in Tsuruoka city. On founding HMT, Otaki and Soga jointly solicited City Hall to open the needed incubator. City Hall officials initially proposed the old City Hospital building as an incubation facility, but it was determined an inappropriate space with its confined rooms and structural pillars. In a bold decision, Mayor Tomizuka pledged to build an incubator with the city's budget close to IAB. This rapid decision by the mayor surprised Otaki, Soga, staff members of HMT, and researchers at IAB, but it demonstrated Tomizuka's strong commitment to commercialize this breakthrough technology and provide a critical, unifying catalyst for the company's management and research specialists. As the first president of HMT, Otaki pursued the "three step growth model" shown in Figure 4.3. First, Otaki actively visited major food processing companies in Japan, seeking a partner for HMT research who might ultimately play the role of "earlyvangelist" assuming this breakthrough technology provided valuable industry solutions.[14] Indeed, this first step successfully identified widespread potential applications for metabolome analysis technology, from food processing to new drug development.

The Annual Conference of the Metabolome Society (founded in Boston in 2004) was held in Tsuruoka, June 20–23, 2005, when HMT was pursuing market validation and partners. International researchers attending the conference attracted the attention of Tsuruoka's press and citizens took note as Agilent Technologies Inc., a top US research-instrument manufacturing company, was licensed to manufacture and sell equipment featuring metabolome analysis technology, fulfilling the second step in the "three-step growth model." As Agilent's metabolome analyzers became widely used,

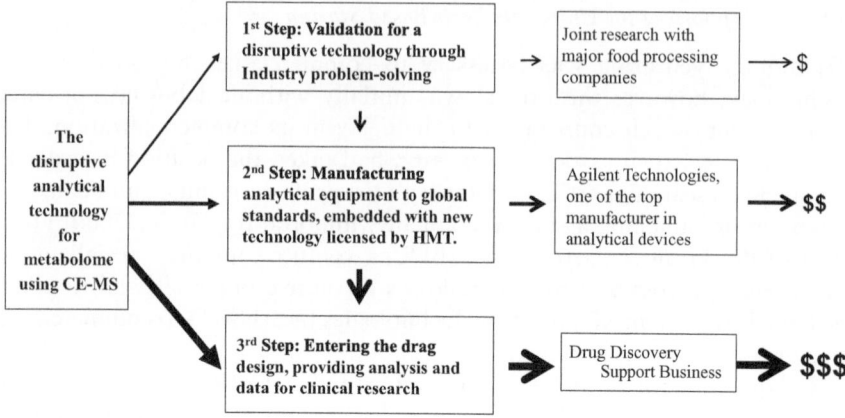

Figure 4.3 Three-Step Growth Strategy of HMT

Source: Authors

Japanese big food manufacturers and other startups moved into the incubator and began collaborating with HMT. These business operations, strategically planned and led by Otaki, resulted in phenomenal growth so that HMT provided return on investment in around five years, avoiding the typical biotech startup scenario requiring large up-front investments over ten or more years. As BFP provided strategic oversight of its financial needs, HMT also established the world's largest metabolome analytical facilities in the Tsuruoka incubator and achieved rapid growth by developing new marker devices for drug design (Figure 4.4). In December 24, 2013, HMT successfully went public in the Tokyo Stock Exchange market, about ten years after its establishment—a remarkable achievement in Japan.

Serving as a "Robust Actor," Tomizuka, the mayor of Tsuruoka city, led these processes by sending clear messages—to IAB, HMT, its supporting partners, City Hall and council, as well as the citizens of Tsuruoka—regarding the importance and usefulness of metabolome R&D activities and the necessity to support HMT by opening an incubator supported through the city's budget, to share the high risk to successfully commercialize HMT. In addition, Tomizuka as the mayor was able to secure the participation of external champions from City Hall, city councilors, academia, and industry as the supporters for HMT through organizing "the Tsuruoka Bio-strategy Roundtable." In addition to the city's budget, Tomizuka actively pursued financial assistance from the Prefecture and Central Governments under supportive "New Capital I" institutions. This strong local support made it possible for Otaki, a biotech venture capitalist, and other academic and industry members to commit to HMT's growth and provide the necessary management resources to commercialize the critically important metabolome analytical technology.[15] Moreover, Tomizuka's efforts motivated

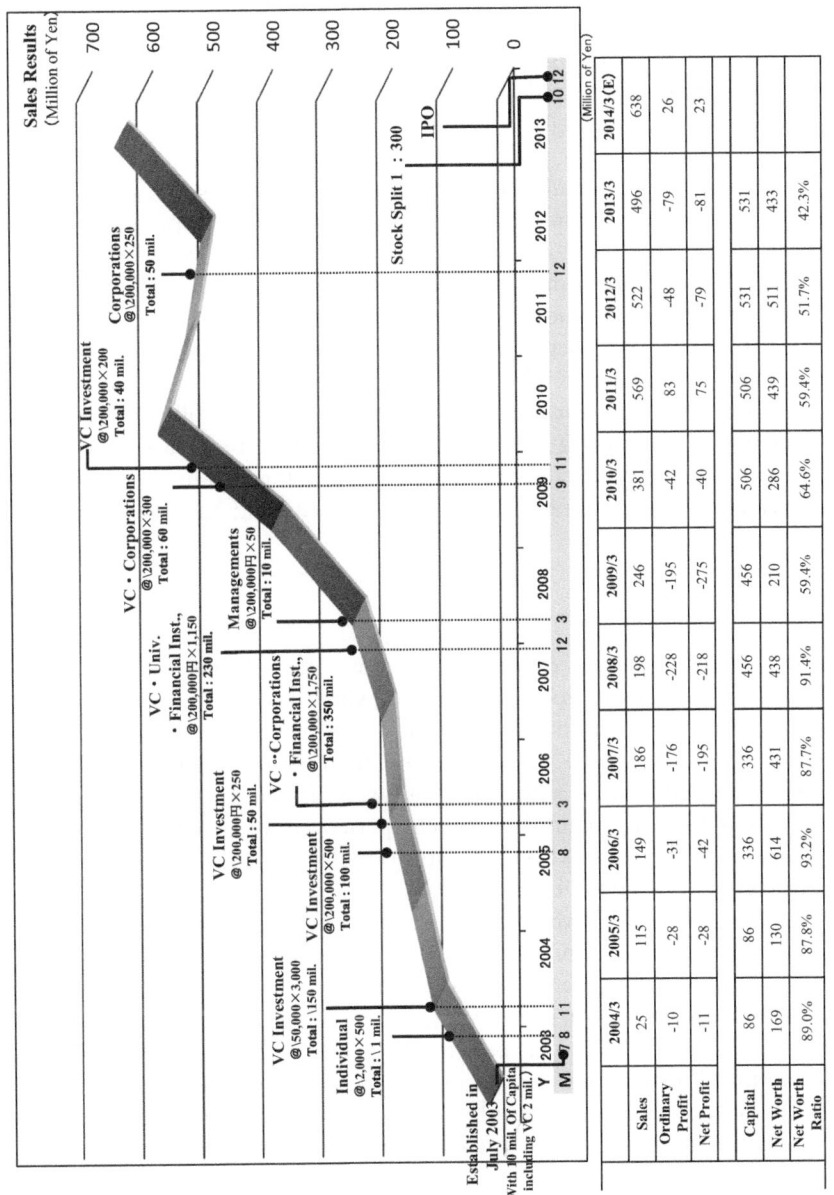

	2004/3	2005/3	2006/3	2007/3	2008/3	2009/3	2010/3	2011/3	2012/3	2013/3	2014/3 (E)
Sales	25	115	149	186	198	246	381	569	522	496	638
Ordinary Profit	-10	-28	-31	-176	-228	-195	-42	83	-48	-79	26
Net Profit	-11	-28	-42	-195	-218	-275	-40	75	-79	-81	23
Capital	86	86	336	336	456	456	506	506	531	531	
Net Worth	169	130	614	431	438	210	286	439	511	433	
Net Worth Ratio	89.0%	87.8%	93.2%	87.7%	91.4%	59.4%	64.6%	59.4%	51.7%	42.3%	

Figure 4.4 Sales & Equity Finance of HMT Co. Ltd.

Source: Prepared by TICC

multiple collaborative academia-industry R&D projects with the goal of commercializing research results. Tomizuka took major risks by first supporting cutting-edge R&D activities at IAB and then establishing an incubator to provide HMT with greater opportunities for success to become "anchor tenant." Importantly, his unwavering consistency inspired the trust of city officials to support his vision.[16] In December 2013, HMT graduated from the incubator as the public high-growth company on Tokyo Stock Exchange Specialized Market.

After being mayor for 18 years, Tomizuka wanted to be succeeded by a younger candidate who would actively support his policies. This mayoral election campaign was countered by a Democratic Party opponent who strongly attacked the Tomizuka's policies supporting tech-based startups. However, despite this stiff opposition, Tomizuka's chosen successor became mayor and did indeed pursue his predecessor's policies. The election result illustrated the broad support among the local inhabitants for Tomizuka's robust actions as influencer with unwavering consistency for a vision for the city's future development that resulted in HMT successfully going public in December 2013. Tomizuka's policy for supporting tech-based startups was formally institutionalized as the city's "Metabolome Industry Creation Policy," which was also supported by Keio University and Yamagata Prefectural Government.

2.4   *Toward Tech-Based Economy*

Tsuruoka's success is seen as exceptional because most of Japan's tech-based entrepreneurial startups are located in Tokyo, where a concentration of talent reflects Japan's policies and mindset.[17] While the Case of Tsuruoka provides a successful regional model to rejuvenate Japan's long-stagnate economy through knowledge-based Technology Venturing, it needs to be stated that other tech-based startups from IAB have experienced long timelines toward success even with the regions similar institutional structure to that in Austin shown in Figure 4.1 (Figure 4.5).

In Japan, as shown in Chapters 1 and 2, the Central Government's "Cloning Silicon Valley Policy" provided both directives and financial support for regions to develop academia-industry R&D collaborations, incubators, VC firms, and specialized quasigovernmental regional development entities. Yet we emphasize that, for such policies to be successful, it is essential for "New Capital I" institutions to be supplemented by regionally based "New Small i" institutions that originate by "robust actors" driving the development of local organizations with a "bottom-up" momentum, rather than by a "top-down" designated policy.

Japanese regional projects have generally been challenged to identify regional champions with the expertise and resources to realize region-wide technology venturing, largely due to an absence of needed visionaries. In Japan, talent gravitates to Tokyo, where tech leaders hope to demonstrate

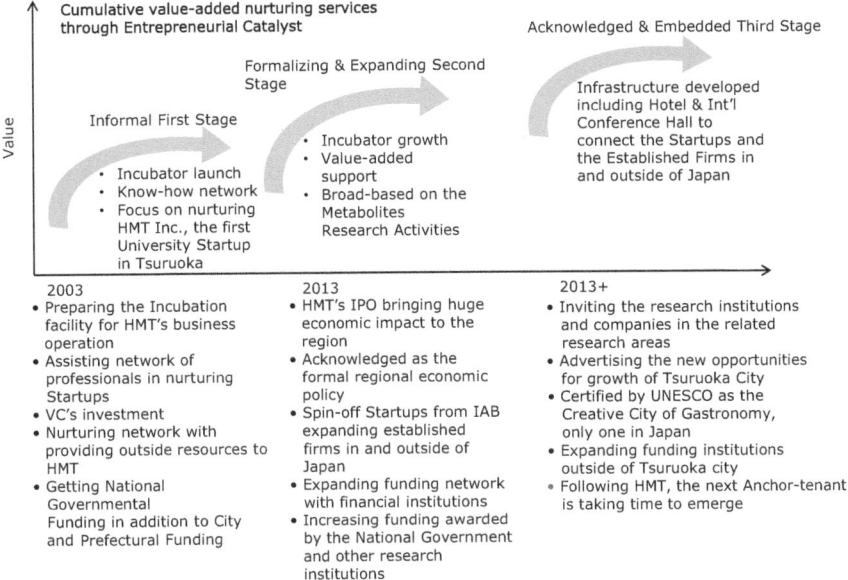

Value

Cumulative value-added nurturing services
through Entrepreneurial Catalyst

Acknowledged & Embedded Third Stage

Formalizing & Expanding Second
Stage

Informal First Stage

Infrastructure developed
including Hotel & Int'l
Conference Hall to
connect the Startups and
the Established Firms in
and outside of Japan

- Incubator launch
- Know-how network
- Focus on nurturing
HMT Inc., the first
University Startup
in Tsuruoka

- Incubator growth
- Value-added
support
- Broad-based on the
Metabolites
Research Activities

2003
- Preparing the Incubation facility for HMT's business operation
- Assisting network of professionals in nurturing Startups
- VC's investment
- Nurturing network with providing outside resources to HMT
- Getting National Governmental Funding in addition to City and Prefectural Funding

2013
- HMT's IPO bringing huge economic impact to the region
- Acknowledged as the formal regional economic policy
- Spin-off Startups from IAB expanding established firms in and outside of Japan
- Expanding funding network with financial institutions
- Increasing funding awarded by the National Government and other research institutions

2013+
- Inviting the research institutions and companies in the related research areas
- Advertising the new opportunities for growth of Tsuruoka City
- Certified by UNESCO as the Creative City of Gastronomy, only one in Japan
- Expanding funding institutions outside of Tsuruoka city
- Following HMT, the next Anchor-tenant is taking time to emerge

Figure 4.5 "New Small i" institution Building in Tsuruoka

Source: Author, made by the material provided by D. Gibson, IC2 at UT Austin, TX, US

their capabilities within Japan's unipolar political and economic structure. In short, Japan faces the true *aporia* that regional Technology Venturing is impeded as the majority of regional talent migrates to Tokyo in pursuit of more diverse and important career opportunities (Nishizawa et al., 2012). Mayor Tomizuka's role in the case of Tsuruoka demonstrates a model, even in Japan, as to how smaller regions can indeed build "New Small i" institutions to meet the specific needs for launching regionally tech-based startups like HMT, from its founding to becoming an "anchor tenant," through the networking of "robust actors" who work together toward a common vision.

An important positive metric suggested by Tsuruoka's case is that high-tech job creation can also result in an increase of in-migration of young talent (aged 25–34). While Tsuruoka's in-migration of young talent is, admittedly, rather small, it is rare in Japan to see a rise in in-migration of young talent in small cities. Furthermore, we suggest that it is difficult to see how young talent recruitment might be sustained as Tokyo's unipolarity continues to expand. Furthermore, Japan as a country has been resistant to recruit and meaningfully involve needed talent from other nations in its universities, established industries, and start-up entrepreneurial culture a big and important difference from US successful technology growth regions like Silicon Valley, Boston 128, and Austin. Nevertheless, Tsuruoka's entrepreneurial successes and talent recruitment successes provide a positive model for other small Japanese cities pursuing tech-based economic growth and where "robust actors" like Mayor Tomizuka might be able to build "New Small i" institutions as an important foundation for tech-based growth.

3   Important Lessons from Austin and Tsuruoka

Feldman and Graddy-Reed (2014, p. 12) state that "in successful high-tech regions there are individuals that assume the role of regional champions who live and work in a region and take responsibility for stewardship of the place." They identify these "dedicated leaders" as being instrumental in building institutions and making connections that transform local economies (2014, p.12). Smilor, Gibson, and Kozmetsky (1989), while studying the development of the Austin Technopolis, proposed the usefulness of the Technopolis Wheel Framework (TWF) composed of a research university; large and emerging businesses; federal, state, and local government; and support groups (Figure 4.6). They locate "Influencers" at the hub as being key to networking and activating commonly unconnected (and perhaps competing) public-private sectors across the TWF.[18] In this context, "Influencers" are seen as regional actors who have exceptional abilities to network across public-private sectors to benefit relationship building that fosters community activities in pursuit of a common vision or regional activity, such as facilitating technology-based economic development.

In 2024, we need to realize that this characterization of "Influencer" was defined decades before the internet and before transformative social media. In future research, it would be interesting to consider the pros and cons of social media networking versus "in-person meetings" for pursuing government, business, and university collaboration and tech-based economic development activities at national and regional levels of analyses. We argue for the importance of in-person networking and relationship building concerning activating regional collaboration across the TWF.[19]

Smilor et al. (1989) and Gibson and Rogers (1994) note that first- and second-level Influencers play different but related roles in fostering community development. While first-level Influencers tend to be quite successful in their primary institutional sectors of employment and interest, they also often maintain significant personal and professional links across regional business, government, and academic sectors. First-level influencers can also identify and motivate a tier of second-level Influencers, who network with credibility and trust across all sectors of the TWF. First-level "Influencers" help inspire and define a unifying vision to motivate specific actions or activities,[20] while second-level "Influencers" act as informal network bridges as they initiate and manage boundary spanning activities, whether within large institutions like the research university or across business and government sectors. First-level Influencers are important in mentoring and, at times, protecting second-level Influencers as they work across institutional boundaries to structure and implement action-oriented activities that at times challenge existing institutionalized norms, rules, procedures, and established expectations of

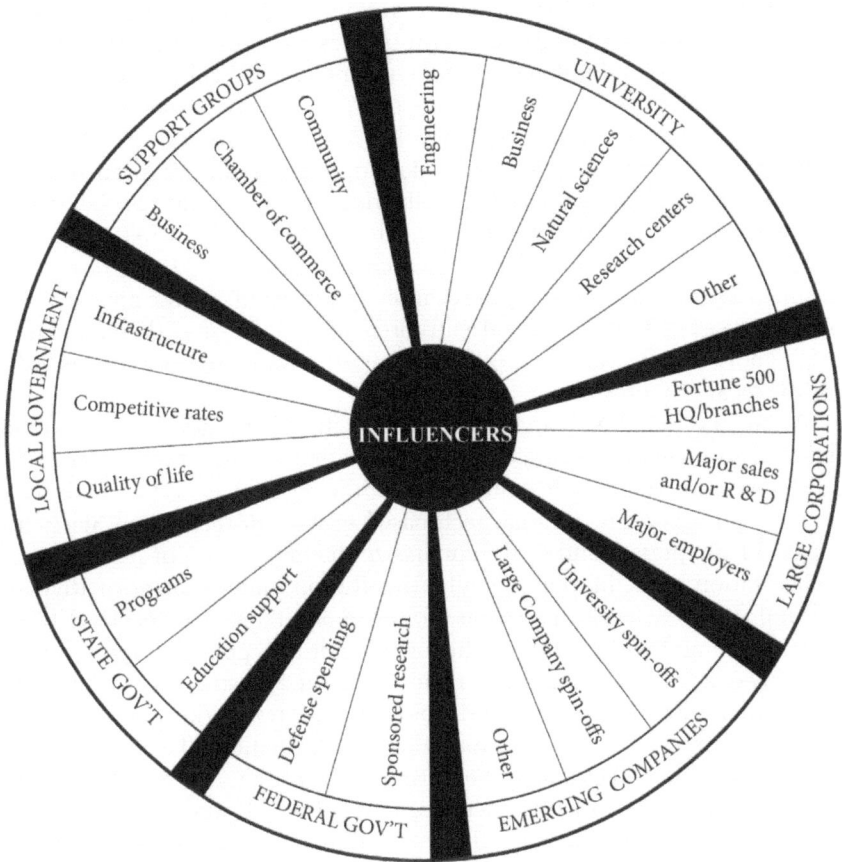

Figure 4.6 Technopolis Wheel Framework
Source: Smilor et al. (1989)

conduct (Gibson & Rogers, 1994; Gibson & Oden, 2019). This networking effect across the TWF helps strengthen "weak ties" on which community and regional opportunities often depend (Granovetter, 1973, 2000, 2018).

In our research, we characterize the successful recruitment of MCC to Austin as the result of effective collaboration and cooperation by academic, business, and government actors at the state and regional levels of analysis. We also emphasized the importance of public-private collaboration in the successful recruitment of technology companies to Austin. In the launch and development of the Austin Technology Incubator (ATI), Kozmetsky showed characteristics that could be defined as a "robust actor," as characterized in Chapter 2; however, we can also identify Kozmetsky as a "Civic Entrepreneur" (Jones, 2018) and first-level Influencer as he worked with UT Austin, the Chamber of Commerce, the City of Austin, and Travis County to financially support and otherwise sustain ATI's successful operation.[21] Kozmetsky's common mode of operation was to enlist the participation of first- and second-level Influencers and encourage their "voluntary" participation on regional projects or programs of interest while promoting a shared vision of activity. In the case of Tsuruoka, Mayor Tomizuka was a first-level Influencer for the region's technology development. As an entrepreneurial and risk-taking politician, rather than following national regulatory-level policies, the mayor inspired and facilitated the establishment of IAB to conduct world-class advanced life science research and education. IAB's researchers invented a breakthrough analysis technology that validated the mayor's belief in the importance of a regional entrepreneurial university, thereby gaining the support of Tsuruoka City and Yamagata Prefecture to promote his vision for the local economy.

We suggest that TWF can serve as a generalizable framework for studying national and regional technology-based growth dynamics. In Chapters 1 and 2, we discuss national policy initiatives, at the regulative level of analysis, to initiate and accelerate regional tech-based growth in the United States and Japan. In Chapters 3 and 4, we emphasize the importance of public-private collaboration in facilitating "Small i" institution building at normative and cultural-cognitive levels of analysis. For example, Tsuruoka—nearly 20 years after Austin and with a different historical, cultural, political, and economic context—was able to establish a regional vision and strategy for launching university R&D and start-ups in the biotech industry working across a range of community sectors. When analyzing the formation of supporting networks to facilitate Technology Venturing in Tsuruoka, it is possible to identify cross-sector networks and actions, some of which were institutionalized as "New Small i" institutions. Table 4.1 illustrates a comparison between Austin and Tsuruoka concerning relevant regional characteristics, "Support Groups" for Technology Venturing and "Influencers" as noted in the TWF.

We emphasize the importance of building "New Small i" institutions consistent with regional context. While our two city regions exhibit different regulative, normative, and cultural-cognitive pillars, in both cases, "Influencers" identified the type of "New Small i" institutions that were necessary to realize successful Technology Venturing and took "robust actions" to create and maintain these institutions. These "Influencers" crossed institutional boundaries to recruit regional supporters to help pursue the goal of tech-based endogenous economic growth supporting their long-term vision. An important ongoing challenge is building a supportive community where in paraphrasing Austin Mayor Lee Cook, "A lot of selfless people do what is needed to make 'their community' a better place for people they had never met and would never know" (Cooke, 2019).

An important conclusion from our comparative analysis of the United States and Japan is that "New Capital I" institutions that initiate well-intended national-level regulative policies are not sufficient and often are not appropriate to launch and sustain successful regional tech-based growth. Importantly,

Table 4.1 Comparison between Austin and Tsuruoka Concerning Relevant Regional Characteristics, "Support Groups" and the Role of "Influencers" as Noted in the TWF

	Austin (1980–1990)	Tsuruoka (2000–2010)
Location	Central Texas, State Capital	Japan Sea side of Tohoku, Old Political City of Edo era
Population	417,000	140,000
Identity	University and State Capital Town not known for technology-based entrepreneurship, businesses, or career possibilities	Old castle town with a fairly conservative rice culture, Tsuruoka was recognized as the United Nations Educational, Scientific, and Cultural Organization (UNESCO) Gastronomy Creative City in 2014 due to its rich food culture.
Cost of living—low for metropolitan areas	Yes	Yes
Environmental features	Located in central Texas, the Austin area is noted for its green hills, pristine lakes, hike and bike trails, and outdoor activities	Tsuruoka is located alongside the Sea of Japan and is noted for its 1400 year old sacred mountains and beautiful forests
Attractive lifestyle of young	"Live Music Capital" "Keep Austin Weird" creative slacker culture and environmental assets attract the young	Young Japanese want to move to bigger city and especially Tokyo for quality jobs and career development
University	UT at Austin theMajor Research University, other regional universities, Austin Community College	IAB of Keio University, Graduate School of University of Tohoku Community Service and Science, Department of Agriculture of Yamagata University (National University)
R&D centers	MCC, SEMATECH	IAB
Support Groups Community		
Incubator	Austin Technology Incubator (ATI)	Tsuruoka Metablome Incubation Center
Co-working spaces/network	Austin Software Council (ASC)	None/Tsuruoka Bio-strategic Council (TBC)
Risk Money Providing System		
Angel network	Texas Capital Network (TCN)	No
Accelerators	ATI	No
VCs	Austin Ventures, Others	Bio-frontier Partners, TICC
Banks	Yes	Shonai Bank (Local Bank headquartered in Tsuruoka)

(Continued)

Table 4.1 (Continued)

	Austin (1980–1990)	Tsuruoka (2000–2010)
Service Providers		
IP law firms	Few	No
Accounting firms	Yes	Few
Securities houses	No	No
Consulting offices	Yes	No
Recruiting offices	Few	No
Advertising firms	Few	No
Other service providers	Yes	No; Inviting experts from Tokyo through TBC as needed
Large corporations	Texas Instruments, IBM, 3M, AMD, Motorola	Mitsukan Vinegar, Ajinomoto, Kirin, RIKEN, Kojima Press
Home grown	TRACOR, Nat'l Instruments, DELL Technologies, Whole Foods	No
Tech-based startups	Software, IT, digital media	Human Metablome Technologies, Spibar, Saliva-tech
Government Policies		
National	University R&D Funding, Bayh-Dole, SBIR, ERISA	Funding University R&D
Regional	State Funding for R&D	Yamagata Prefecture Funding for High-tech R&D
Local	City support for tech-based growth waivers on negative environmental and cost of living impacts	City Funding to IAB Faculties and Operation
Influencers		
First level	G. Kozmetsky: IC2 Institute, UT Austin P. Powers: Executive Assistant to Texas Governor M. White	Y. Tomizuka, Mayer (1991–2009)
Second level	Laura Kilcrease, Director of ATI Glenn West President of Greater Austin Chamber of Commerce (GACC)	Dr. M. Tomita, Director of IAB; Officials of City Hall; Dr. Y. Ohtaki; Bio-technology Venture Capitalist Dr. Miyata, Specialist in Bio-technology industry

Source: Authors.

specific outcomes of "New Capital I" policies at the regulative level as formal policy can NOT *a priori* be tested at the regional level (Feld, 2012). While "Capital I" institutions can introduce and enact policies backed by laws and regulations, "Small i" institutions require bottom-up efforts and the robust actions, creativity, and energy of regional influencers. Therefore, we stress the importance of including regionally based first- and second-level Influencers in designing regional-level initiatives, both for their insight and to secure their engagement and energy in implementing these initiatives. We believe that one of the most important lessons from the Austin and Tsuruoka cases is that regional "Influencers" are key actors who can effectively link "Capital I" institution initiatives with "New Small i" institutional support for successful technology-based economic development.[22]

Notes

1 *The American Growth Report*, October 2022, ranked Austin as the second fastest growth US city with the metro population of 2,176,000. San Francisco, CA, is ranked first. An interesting way to assess the relative tech-based growth and impact of these two regions is to consider business development in the current high interest area of AI (Artificial Intelligence). Austin saw 264 generative AI job postings in the greater Austin region as noted in a 2023 Brookings analysis while the Bay Area and Silicon Valley, by contrast, had nearly 3,000 such job postings the same year. Still, in describing how AI had become the subject of economic competition across the US, the Brookings Industry Report named Austin as one of the early adopter cities of artificial intelligence technology and described how "Austin is clearly in the tier of maybe 10 places that are the next ring out from the Bay Area, which is the unquestioned superstar center of all this," Mark Muro, lead author of the Brookings 2023 report, told Axios ("Austin's Artificial Intelligence Boom," Asher Price, Axios, Austin News, February 2, 2024).

2 As mentioned in Chapter 1, Japan's "Cloning Silicon Valley Policy" established "Industrial Clustering Policy" to promote regional expansion in 18 city regions (see Notes 22 and 23). Although there was a major electronics company's semiconductor production plant located in Tsuruoka, there were no leading research institutions, including universities, located in the area, and thus, Tsuruoka was not selected as a candidate site for technology cluster formation under "Industrial Clustering Policy."

3 The University of Texas was founded in Austin in 1883 as the flagship campus of the University of Texas System which, as of 2024, includes eight universities and five health institutions. However, nearly 140 years ago, The University began operations with one building, eight professors, and 221 students. As of 2024, UT-Austin ranks among the top 40 universities in the world with an enrollment of 52,000 students, 3,000 teaching faculty, and educational and research programs across 19 colleges and schools and more than 200 dedicated research units and centers. As Texas' leading research university, UT-Austin is supported by annual research funding of about $650 million. Several research groups report directly to the Vice President for Research, Scholarship and Creative Endeavors, but most research and educational units are based in individual colleges and schools, where they engage in interdisciplinary research that complements the academic goals of their departments.

4 Indeed, in this regard, The University of Texas at Austin scored an academic coup that had a major impact on faculty recruiting among the nation's top research

universities. Peter O'Donnell, Jr. a wealthy Texan who lived in Dallas was impressed with Austin's winning MCC and Texas' drive to become a world competitor in high technology. After conferring with MCC and Texas business and academic leaders he decided to give UT-Austin $8 million to fund academic chairs in science. O'Donnell's gift was matched by an additional $8 million in donations from the private sector throughout Texas (to total $16 million) and as part of UT-Austin's Centennial Program this $16 M was matched by the UT System University's Permanent University Fund (PUF) to establish 32 endowed chairs at UT-Austin in the colleges of natural science and engineering (Gibson and Rogers, 1994: p. 446).

5 It is important to note that during his career as Dean of UT Austin's College and Graduate School of Business and Founding Director of IC² Institute, George Kozmetsky was the go-to mentor for many of Austin's emerging and established business and civic entrepreneurs. Most notably this list included Jim Truchard at National Instruments in the late 1970s and Michael Dell at PC's Limited in the early 1980s.

6 These statistics (which continue to accrue over time) were taken from the ATI website in March 2024. www.ati.utexas.edu.

7 This research was performed in support of IC² Institute research, "Austin Innovation and Collaboration Spaces," by J. Spencer and D. Gibson.

8 *The Entrepreneurial University: Context and Institutional Change* (2015) Foss and Gibson (eds.): presents eight cases assessing the regional economic impact of universities in the following four countries: Norway, Finland, the United Kingdom, and the United States. Each of the case authors present an in-depth analysis of the entrepreneurial transition of "their" university and regional economy toward fostering and accelerating tech-based growth. The universities and regions vary in size, wealth, and entrepreneurial development success. The research framework features "Entrepreneurial Architecture" as defined by Vorley and Nelles (2009) which refers to five variables that interact to shape regional entrepreneurial agendas: Structures (i.e., tech parks and incubators), Systems (i.e., networks of communication, Leadership (i.e., orientation of key influencers), Strategies (i.e., policy), and Culture (i.e., attitudes and norms). In their concluding chapter, editors Foss and Gibson assess the importance of the five indicators that were referenced in each case, and they ranked them in terms of importance in attaining successful entrepreneurial transition of the universities and regions. The most important predictor was university and regional culture followed by leadership capability followed by system networks and strategies, and the least important was structures. Even within the smallest and most homogeneous countries like Norway and Finland, university and regional culture was considered the dominant variable in predicting entrepreneurial transition success when compared to the other four architecture variables.

9 *Austin City Limits* (ACL) began in 1974 as a live music television program produced by Austin PBS initially at UT Austin's College of Communication. ACL remains the only television show to receive the National Medal of Arts, awarded in 2003, and an institutional Peabody Award, awarded in 2011 "for its more than three decades of presenting and preserving eclectic American musical genres." ACL also hosts an Austin City Limits Fall music festival in Austin's Zilker Park. Another major nationally and internationally known Austin-based performance-oriented annual conference is South by SouthwestSXSW. Launched by Austin entrepreneurs in 1987 as a music festival for largely local performers, SXSW has grown to include film screenings, interactive media, and topical education panels. Although a rather large event with attendance totaling approximately 417,400, SXSW could be considered an important "Small i" networking institution in that it makes possible national and international networking opportunities for performers, innovative companies, and entrepreneurs.

10 Japan's transistor production had been rapidly expanding since the late 1960s, and it was inevitable for major manufacturers such as NEC to hire incoming female talent, many of whom were from Yamagata Prefecture. Therefore, NEC decided to set up its first regional plant in Takahata-machi, Yamagata Prefecture, and with the extensive cooperation of the local community, the move was a success. To further expand this trend, NEC Yamagata added a plant specializing in semiconductor wafer and other facilities in Tsuruoka. In 1976, NEC Yamagata moved its headquarters to Tsuruoka, which became the center of NEC semiconductor production.

11 The ASEAN is currently comprised of ten nations: Brunei, Cambodia, Indonesia, Laos, Malaysia, Myanmar, the Philippines, Singapore, Thailand, and Vietnam. The association seeks to "accelerate economic growth, social progress, and cultural development in the region, to promote regional peace, collaboration and mutual assistance on matters of common interest, to provide assistance to each other in the form of training and research facilities, to collaborate for better utilization of agriculture and industry to raise the living standards of the people, to promote Southeast Asian studies and to maintain close, beneficial co-operation with existing international organizations with similar aims and purposes." Source: Wikipedia, https://en.wikipedia.org/wiki/ASEAN as archived from *"The Asean Declaration (Bangkok Declaration) Bangkok, 8 August 1967."*

12 IAB's operating costs were (1) 4.5 billion yen for the first period (2001–2005) focusing on the fundamental research, (2) 3.5 billion yen for the second period (2006–2010) focusing on development research, (3) 2.1 billion yen for the third period (2011–2013) focusing on applied research, and (4) 2.1 billion yen for 2014–2017, with future amounts to be determined, based on the research's results (*Nikkei Newspaper*, 2014). In terms of sharing the financial burden, Yamagata Prefecture covered 45% and the city of Tsuruoka paid 55%. It was extraordinary in Japan that the city bore much of the cost of R&D activities, including researchers' salaries for such a long period. However, it was not possible for the Central Government to provide perpetual support for regional salaries and research for these specific technologies in this area due to the National Fiscal Regulations.

13 After acquiring a doctoral degree from Tohoku University, Dr. Otaki joined the Nomura Life Sciences, a subsidiary of Nomura Research Institute (NRI), and expanded his career in the life sciences arena through providing toxicity tests to major drug companies in Japan belonging to the neutral third-party institution. However, even though NRI was a leading research institute in Japan, the organization closed—unable to maintain the high cost of life science research activities. Otaki fulfilled expectations by transferring to JAFCO, another Nomura group leading VC, where he accumulated important expertise in overseeing investment in European and American biotech startups. While Otaki diverged from the Japanese norm of pursuing a single-company career after securing a degree, his career path is comparable to the experiences of venture capitalists in the United States. In 1999, he opened the venture capital firm BFP with excellent investment performances including MedGene (now AnGes MG, Inc.), a biotech startup company that emerged from research at Osaka University, and has been involved in developing the life science policies of the Ministry of Health, Labor and Welfare, and the Ministry of Education, Culture, Sports and Technology.

14 This can be defined to be the similar nascent R&D supporting finance measure as "Science-for-Hire." While "Science-for-Hire" commonly refers to "Research and Development activities conducted for another party on a contractual basis," it is appreciated as "an important vehicle for financing startups, as nascent R&D is difficult to finance with any type of funding." In the United States, "many technology entrepreneurs support the preliminary development of technology through participation in federally funded R&D programs" which provided "Science-for-Hire" R&D activities under the Small Business Innovation Research

(SBIR), Small Business Technology Transfer (STTR), and Advance Technology Program (ATP) institutionalized as "New Capital I" (Servo, 2005). Unfortunately, the Japanese version of SBIR cannot provide direct funding to tech-based startups, but only subsidies in the form of matching grants. Consequently, Otaki sought opportunities with private companies, functioning as "Science-for-Hire." He succeeded in finding good results with the vinegar brewer, Mizkan Corp., one of the old food processing companies in Japan, which sought scientific evidence for its products' health benefits. New metabolome analytical technology was able to provide this evidence clearly through cellular analysis of the vinegar's components and effects. The proposal was accepted to analyze the results of its product in the cells of human body, which secured "Science-for-Hire" for HMT's R&D activities.

15 In Japan, expert committees at the national and local levels commonly authorize bureaucratic decisions and policies, yet the participating experts are not held accountable for their comments, nor do they commit to the content of their statements. "The Tsuruoka Bio-strategy Round-table," however, operated in a completely different manner, as Tomizuka implemented the recommendations of the experts and verified the results. Therefore, the participants took their roles seriously as they recommended specific measures to support HMT's growth, making this organization an unprecedented committee of experts.

16 Anecdotally, when Tomizuka attended the screening committee at Kasumigaseki to receive funding from Japanese Central Government, he proposed a fact-based reform plan to accurately support regional realities—which went against the advice given by bureaucrats of the Central Government. This flouted the expectation that, when seeking funds, local government officials at the mayoral level were expected to accept the Central Government's offerings without objection. But City Hall officials attending with Tomizuka later said that they so fully agreed with Tomizuka's refutation, and they no longer cared whether they were awarded Central Government funding. This anecdote illustrates Tomizuka's unique capacity to grasp current situations and economic futures, a quality that Tsuruoka's City Hall officials understood and highly appreciated.

17 A prefecture-by-prefecture comparison of startup funding data shows Tokyo with 653.1 billion yen and a growing national share of 83.7, with Kanagawa in second place at 3.1%, Kyoto at 2.1%, Yamagata at 2.0%, Fukuoka at 1.9%, and all others combined at 7.2%. Yamagata Prefecture's high percentage is due to funding from startup companies in Tsuruoka (INITIAL, *2021 Japan Startup Finance*, Uzabase, 2022).

18 Mazzucato (2014) points out that the Innovation System and Innovation Ecosystem theories assume the myth that related organizations and associations, or public-private organizational partnerships, can work together symbiotically; however, in reality, there are conflicts of interest and parasitic relationships. The point that the TWF clarifies is that "Influencers" play a critical role to bringing organizations and institutions together working to build collaborative activity and symbiotic relationships.

19 It is interesting to consider the role and meaning of "Influencer" before the existence of the internet and social media. In a February 2024 interview with Jim Butler, a former Texas state government employee during Governor Ann Richards's administration 1991–1995. At the time, Jim was in charge of multimedia development for the state of Texas, and he remembered being asked by the Governor to meet with George Kozmetsky at his IC[2] Institute office. It seems Dr. Kozmetsky had called Governor Richards asking to meet with a state employee knowledgeable about multimedia development in South Texas. Richard's office contacted the head of the State's economic development which

identified Jim Butler, Manager of Multimedia Development for the State, as the best person to meet with Dr. Kozmetsky. The meeting was scheduled for 5:30 AM, as early morning was when George Kozmetsky (GK) preferred to meet and explore new ideas and network connections concerning topics of interest. In the meeting with Butler, Kozmetsky wanted to know about multimedia business development on state's southern border with Mexico in regard to a project he was championing with UT Brownsville and Texas Southmost College on the launching of The Cross-Boder Institute for Regional Development (CBIRD). The focus was how these universities along with IC² Institute and working with Brownsville and Matamoros city's academic, business, and government sectors could facilitate cross-border entrepreneurial economic development, education, and research in targeted areas of concern such as manufacturing and maquiladoras, transportation and logistics, health services, and immigration and border security. Jim Butler met with Kozmetsky on several mornings providing contact information and knowledge on multimedia business and research activities with possible links to the border. Jim was impressed with Kozmetsky's vision and passion for the CBIRD project. But, as he remembered, "there were lots of wheels spinning with GK all the time and at times I wasn't sure what we were talking about." Kozmetsky commonly worked with a "white board" to diagram important aspects of his early morning in-person discussions. After each of their meetings, Jim would ask Kozmetsky to provide him with a clear summary of what they had discussed, so he would have a good understanding of what they were taking about and what Kozmetsky wanted him to tell his boss and Governor Richards.

20 A central first-level Influencer in Austin, George Kozmetsky, was an accomplished entrepreneur,,university researcher, and academic dean, while, in Tsuruoka's case, Mayor Tomizuka was known as an entrepreneurial and risk-taking politician. Instead of following national regulatory-level policies, Tsuruoka's Mayor inspired and facilitated the establishment of IAB to conduct "world-class" advanced life science research and education. IAB's researchers invented a breakthrough analysis technology that validated the mayor's belief in the importance of a regional entrepreneurial university, thereby gaining the support of Tsuruoka City and Yamagata Prefecture to promote this vision for the local economy.

21 We can identify the concept of "Influencers" with "Civic Entrepreneurs" who organize communities for new economic growth (Henton et al., 1997) or as "Institutional Entrepreneurs" who engage in entrepreneurial activities to build new institutions (Scott, 2014). However, these concepts refer only to the actions of specific individuals and cannot be said to reveal the specific activities of building "New Small i" institutions in Austin and elsewhere. Auerswald and Branscomb (2003) introduced the term "collective entrepreneurship" as being encouraged to participate in "trust- and reputation-based" nurturing activities for realizing Technology Venturing, in which not only private equity investors but also supporters from Academic-Industry-Government (AIG) sectors, called as "external champions," can be organized. By presenting the specific activities of regional "Influencers," we intend to clarify the content of the term "collective entrepreneurship."

22 Feldman and Zoller (2012) demonstrate that dealmakers contributed to the development of "entrepreneurial economies" by providing social capital through actor-networks in entrepreneurial economies across the United States such as Boston R128 and Silicon Valley. At the same time, they point out that a long-term analysis of organizing actor-networks is needed for defining unique acts such as boundary spanning as exhibited by dealmakers.

References

ASEAN (1967). The ASEAN Declaration (Bangkok Declaration). Bangkok, August 8.

ATLAS (2022). "Dr. George Kozmetsky: The Visionary Who Shaped Austin Technology Industry" Academy of Transdisciplinary Learning and Advanced Studies (ATLAS) website. https://www.theatlas.org/index.php?option=com_content&view=article&layout=edit&id=301. Accessed October, 2022.

Auerswald, P. E. & L. M. Branscomb (2003). "Start-ups and Spin-offs: Collective Entrepreneurship between Invention and Innovation," pp. 61–91, in D. M. Hart (Eds.), *The Emergence of Entrepreneurship Policy*. Cambridge, UK: Cambridge University Press.

Avnimelech, G. & M. P. Feldman (2010). "Regional Corporate Spawning and the Role of Homegrown Companies," *Review of Policy Research*, 27(4), 475–489.

Cooke, L. (2019). Personal interview by D. V. Gibson, May 30.

Cooper, A. C. (1985). "The Role of Incubator Organizations in the Founding of Growth-oriented Firms," *Journal of Business Venturing*, 1(1), 75–86.

Dell, M. & C. Fredman (1999). *Direct from Dell: Strategies That Revolutionized an Industry*. New York: Harper Business.

Dell, M. & J. Kaplan (2021). *Play Nice but Win: A CEO's Journey from Founder to Leader*. New York: Portfolio/Penguin.

Echeverri-Carroll, E. L., M. D. Oden, D. V. Gibson & E. A. Johnston (2018). "Unintended Consequences on Gender Diversity of High-tech Growth and Labor Market Polarization," *Research Policy*, (47)1, February, 209–217.

Epstein, L. (2019). Email correspondence to D. V. Gibson, May 2.

Feld, B. (2012). *Startup Communities: Building an Entrepreneurial Ecosystem in Your City*. Hoboken, NJ: Wiley & Sons.

Feldman, M. P. & T. D. Zoller (2012). "Dealmakers in Place: Social Capital Connections in Regional Entrepreneurial Economies," *Regional Studies*, 46(1), 23–37.

Feldman, M. P. & A. Graddy Reed (2014). "Local Champions: Entrepreneurs' Transition to Philanthropy and the Vibrancy of Place," Chapter 3 pp. 43–72, in M. L. Taylor, R. J. Strom & D. O. Renz (Eds.), *Handbook of Research on Entrepreneurs' Engagement in Philanthropy*. Northampton, MA: Edgar Elgar.

Florida, R. (2002). *The Rise of the Creative Class*. New York: Basic Books.

Gibbons, M., M. Trow, P. Scott, S. Schwartzman, H. Nowotny & C. Limoges (1994). "The New Production of Knowledge: The Dynamics of Science and Research in Contemporary Societies," *Contemporary Sociology*, 24(6). DOI: 10.2307/20 76669.

Gibson, D. V. & E. Rogers (1994). *R&D Collaboration on Trial: The Microelectronics and Computer Technology Corporation*. Boston, MA: Harvard Business School Press.

Gibson, D. V. & M. Oden (2019). "The Launch and Evolution of a Technology-based Economy: The Case of Austin Texas," pp. 1–22, *Growth and Change*, 50(3). Wiley Periodicals, Inc.

Granovetter, M. S. (1973). "The Strength of Weak Ties," *American Journal of Sociology*, Vol. 78, Issue 6, 1360–1380.

Granovetter, M. (2000). "The Economic Sociology of Firms and Entrepreneurs," *University of Illinois at Urbana-Champaign's Academy for Entrepreneurial Leadership Historical Research Reference in Entrepreneurship*.

Granovetter, M. (2018). *Getting a Job: A Study of Contacts and Careers*. Chicago, IL: University of Chicago Press.

Henton, D., J. Melville & K. Walesh (1997). *Grassroot Leaders: How Civic Entrepreneurs Are Building Prosperous Communities*. San Francisco, CA: Jossey-Bass Publishers.

Ishida, H. (2014). *Case-book V: Entrepreneurs Who Change Region and Society* [in Japanese]. Tokyo: Keio University Press.

Jones, M. (2018). *A Civic Entrepreneur: The Life of Technology Visionary George Kozmetsky*. Austin, TX: Tower Books.

Kanter, R. (1985). "Supporting Innovation and Venture Development in Established Companies," *Journal of Business Venturing*, 2(1), 47–60.

Kenney, M. (Ed.) (2000). *Understanding Silicon Valley: The Anatomy of an Entrepreneurial Region*. Stanford, CA: Stanford University Press.

Klepper, S. (2010). "The Origin and Growth of Industry Clusters: The Making of Silicon Valley and Detroit," *Journal of Urban Economics*, (67)1, January, 15–32.

Kozmetsky, G. (1993). "Breaking the Mold: Reinventing Business through Community Collaboration," paper delivered at the MIT Enterprise Forum.

Ladendorf, K. (1997). "Fort Worth Hits It Big," *Austin American-Statesman*, March 19, D-19.

Marshall, A. (1986). *Principles of Economics*, 8th Edition. New York: Macmillan.

Masuda, H. (Ed.) (2014). *Disappearing Regions in Japan* [in Japanese]. Tokyo: Chuou Kouron-sha.

Mazzucato, M., (2014). *The Entrepreneurial State*, London" Anthem Press.

Nikkei Newspaper (2015). February 5, Tohoku Area-version.

Nishizawa, A. et al. (2012). *Regional Ecosystem Creating High-tech Industries* [in Japanese]. Japan: Yuhikaku.

Oden, M. & B. Yilmaz (2005). "From Assembly to Innovation: Learning from the Birth and Development of a High-tech Region," *Workshop on Science City Governance*, UNESCO-WTA Project Steering Committee (pp. 93–130). Daejeon.

Perryman, M. R. (2021). *The Power of Powers IV*. In syndication, November 3.

Schoar, A. (2010). "The Divide between Subsistence and Transformational Entrepreneurship" in J. Lerner & S. Stern (Eds.), *Innovation Policy and the Economy* (pp. 57–81). Chicago, IL: University of Chicago Press.

Scott, W. R. (2014). *Institutions and Organizations: Ideas, Interests, and Identities*, 4th Edition. Thousand Oaks, CA: Sage Publications.

Servo, J. C. (2005). *Business Planning for Scientists & Engineers*, 4th Edition. Galveston, TX: Dawnbreaker.

Smilor, R. W., D. V. Gibson & G. Kozmetsky (1989). "Creating the Technopolis: High-technology Development in Austin, Texas," *Journal of Business Venturing*, 4(1), 49–67.Sivianidou, R. & K. Polenske (1988). "Assessing Regional Economic Impacts with Microcomputers," *Journal of the American Planning Association*, 54(1), 101–106. https://doi.org/10.1080/01944368808977160

Soga, T. (2004). "Metabolome Research: Large-Scale Analysis of IntracellularMetabolites Using CE-MS [in Japanese]," pp. 1–4, *TAITEC Magazine*, 12, TAITEC Co. Ltd., Saitama, Japan.

Storper, M. (2013). *Keys to the City: How Economics, Institutions, Social Interaction, and Politics Shape Development*. Princeton, NJ: Princeton University Press.

Storper, M., T. Kemeny, N. Makarem & T. Osman (2015). *The Rise and Fall of Urban Economies: Lessons from San Francisco and Los Angeles.* Redwood City, CA: Stanford University Press.
Vorley, T. & J. Nelles (2009). "Building Entrepreneurial Architectures: A Conceptual Interpretation of the Third Mission," *Policy Futures in Education,* 7(3), 284–296.
West, G. (2016). Personal interview by D. V. Gibson, March 16.
West, G. (2019). Email correspondence to D. V. Gibson, May 3.
Wilson, M. (2016). Email correspondence to D. V. Gibson, February 1.

5 Conclusion

Important Conditions for Successful Endogenous Tech-Based Economic Development

Our research objective in this book is to clarify important determinants in launching and sustaining successful tech-based endogenous economic development. We employ regulative, normative, and cultural-cognitive levels of analysis to examine institutional perspectives and policy initiatives at the national level in the United States and Japan as well as at the regional level though comparative analysis of Austin, Texas, and Tsuruoka, Japan. In our comparative analysis, we focus on the early stages of regional tech-based economic growth and the important role of "Robust Actors" and "Influencers" in designated organizational fields of activity. Our intention is to provide theoretically sound and useful recommendations for achieving tech-based economic development and growth across a broad range of developed and developing nations and regions.

While we discuss the importance of "New Capital I" institutions at the regulatory level of analysis and "New Small i" institutions at the normative and cultural-cognitive levels of analysis, a lack of appreciation regarding the complementarity between these levels has led to controversy concerning, what we suggest, is the overemphasized importance of macro-policy's impact on regional tech-based entrepreneurial growth. For example, as Mazzucato (2014) emphasizes the value of "New Capital I" institutions as evidenced by her focus on Small Business Innovation Research (SBIR) programs, while McClosky and Mingardi (2020, p. 118) emphasize the importance of regionally based institutions as being crucial to successful technology venturing. O'Conner et al. (2018) note the emergence of a place-based perspective on high-tech industry formation as represented by Entrepreneurial Ecosystems theory.[1] North (1990) emphasizes the importance of informal institutions relative to Storper's (2013) focus on the key importance of regionally based mezzo-level institutions. However, even though informal constraints on institutions are commonly recognized as key to analyzing and achieving successful Entrepreneurial Ecosystems (EEs) researchers tend to exclude these variables from analysis, noting that EEs are extremely difficult to observe as they depend on people's attitudes and beliefs, which are difficult to measure (Fuentelsaz et.al., 2018, p. 52).

DOI: 10.4324/9781003488149-6

In our comparative research on Austin and Tsuruoka we elaborate Storper's (2013) research which stresses the importance of local context, or *genius*, as the source of the uniqueness of "New Small i" institutions. However, focusing on the importance of regional mezzo-level institutions should not lead to a lack of attention policy initiatives at macro-level "New Capital I" institutions concerning regional high-tech industry development.[2] In the cases of Boston R128 and Silicon Valley, "New Capital I" institutions at the federal level including DOD (Department of Defense) and NASA (National Aeronautics and Space Administration) funded breakthrough research and development (R&D) provided an important catalyst to entrepreneurial universities and regionally based "Robust Actors" crucial to achieving successful technology venturing and innovative technology development. One of the main conclusions of this book is the importance of having a synergistic relationship between "New Capital I" and "New Small i" institutions.

An additional intent of our comparative research on Austin and Tsuruoka is to discuss the importance of local context, or culture, in the building regionally appropriate "New Small i" institutions. It is not that Tsuruoka should try to become more like Austin just as Austin has not tried or indeed wanted to be like Silicon Valley. We support the view that regions should assess and build on their own unique strengths to overcome their own unique developmental and community and industry building challenges. The generalizable context that we see as important to all regions is the building and sustaining "Small i" institutions that fit with local realities, culture, and context. In demonstrating the formation of "Startup Community" as an "Entrepreneurial Ecosystem" in Boulder, Colorado, Feld (2012, p. 34) argues that while "context" inspires people to form such a community, it fails to specify the specifics. In our comparative research, we identify the "specifics" of local context in the building of "New Small i" institutions in Austin and Tsuruoka.

To better understand and clarify the specific roles of "Influencers" who initiate the building of "New Small i" institutions, we note the importance of the vision of first-level "Influencers" such as G. Kozmetsky in Austin and Y. Tomizuka in Tsuruoka, as well as second-level "Influencers" in both regions research universities, large and small firms; different levels of government; and support groups composing each sector of the Technopolis Wheel Framework (TWF). We observe that "Influencers" who cross organizational and institutional boundaries are crucial to building "New Small i" institutions and support networks and ultimately to achieving regional tech-based economic growth. In our analysis of Austin and Tsuruoka, two city regions composed of considerably different cultural and political contexts, we illustrate generalizable causalities and the importance of "New Small i" institution building processes. We find that the role of "Influencer" corresponds nicely with the role of "actor" as specified in Scott's (2014) "Top-Down and Bottom-Up Processes of Institutional Creation and Diffusion" providing a useful lens for the specialized functions and roles across the TWF in building "New

Small i" institutions. We refer to the "Organization Field Model" as a useful way to elucidate theoretical causal relationships in networks of concern that are important to Technology Venturing. We observe, however, that even when "New Small i" institutions are considered important for tech-based regional economic development, they often do not receive active broad-based community support, at least initially. Accordingly, "New Small i" institutionalization activities benefit from demonstrating visible outcomes such as growing successful "Anchor Tenants" that provide positive economic benefits to the region, thereby helping to gain "Collective Rationality." We refer to the importance of negotiation and "Collective Rationality" in establishing "New Small i" organizations to mentor entrepreneurs, to share the burden of risk in Technology Venturing, to establish normative recognition, and to gain social legitimacy. We emphasize that although content and character of "New Small i" institutions may vary by regional context, there is a commonality in the important role of "Influencers" who conceive of and build "New Small i" institutions consistent with regional context.

Our comparative analysis of only two cases—one in the United States and the other in Japan—cannot be considered conclusive validation for our thesis, but hopefully it provides useful insights and recommendations for enhancing regional economic development from both theoretical and practical perspectives. In this regard, we hope that the Organization Field Model applied to the TWF and Technology Venturing provides useful perspectives on "New Capital I" and "New Small i" institutional building processes, while accepting the importance of local context, or *genius*, as proposed by Storper (2013) as well as the importance of "informal constraints of institutions" as presented by North (1990). In the cases of Austin and Tsuruoka (despite vastly different cultures and contexts), we recognize common causalities in the formation of "New Small i" institutions based on the pivotal role of "Influencers" who provide inspirational leadership and work toward a consistent, clear vision of activity. It is our hope that our analysis of place-based economic growth in the transformative era of digital technology growth will inspire additional research regarding the importance and function of institutions in regional economic development as well as the roles of "Robust Actors" and "Influencers" in a broad range of regional cultural and policy contexts. We hope that this analysis might inspire challenged regions to reach beyond the boundaries of siloed institutions to identify community leaders across public-private sectors and together to pursue transformational regional change and in the building of needed community.

We recognize both the urgency and the complexity that is inherent to global challenges of building economies that can generate the employment, financial resources, and human talent needed to effectively address the looming challenges of climate change, aging infrastructure, the migration of human talent from challenged regions, and income inequality. We suggest that the underlying philosophy of institution-based community activity advocated in this book is the same orientation that is needed to successfully address these important challenges even while we recognize that many communities of the world are challenged in ways that limit their capacity to pursue or even seriously consider regional economic development and growth. Haskel and Westlake (2022) note that "The Great Economic Disappointment and Its Symptoms," emerging at the beginning of the 21st century, resulted from the inability to successfully build institutions to accommodate disruptive new technologies. We have seen in our comparative analysis of Austin and Tsuruoka, that even well-intended national-level regulative policies will not produce the desired economic growth if they do not complement or at least appreciate regional context. Accordingly, we argue the importance for public-private networks formed and activated at the regional level to shape action initiatives to enhance the success of place-based industrial policy.

The Brookings Institution report (Atkinson et al., 2019) identified the need for place-based industrial policy and a reduction in regional disparities caused by the digital technological revolution that began in the1980s. In this regard, we believe that regional development through building "New Small i" institutions in consort with "New Capital I" institutions is important to achieving successful industrial policy. Worldwide, regional and income disparities are increasing while overall wealth is growing in macroeconomic terms. To help address this disparity, the Biden administration implemented Build Back Better (BBB) Regional Challenge policy and new economic revitalizing macro-policies seeking to revitalize regional economies through tech-based economic growth. We suggest BBB Regional Challenge policy will be more effective if regional "Influencers" are enabled to build "New Small i" institutions that reflect and support diverse US and international regional contexts. It would be our great pleasure if this book might contribute to the development of theoretically and practically viable models for R&D driven tech-based endogenous economic development across national and cultural boundaries.

Notes

1 A biological analogy applied to ecosystems attempts to present the environmental conditions where tech-based entrepreneurial start-ups can thrive and cluster resulting in formation of high-tech industry (Cavallo, et al., 2018: pp. 11–12). However, in reality, it is difficult to use the ecosystem concept to analyze a specific region such as Silicon Valley. To address this difficulty, Doss and Brett (2015) developed a *Scorecard* applying a rainforest analogy to the innovative entrepreneurial organizations that thrive in Silicon Valley. However, as Storper (2013) notes, such studies of regional context have become the "Dark Matter" of economics since the theoretical analysis of regional context has largely been inadequate because it "has been mostly relegated to the black box of cultural differences" (p. 152). To overcome the limitations of Entrepreneurial Ecosystem theory, which has received much attention but has yet to produce concrete results of high-tech industries formation we believe that an institutional perspective is useful to analyze the "Dark Matter" that Storper emphasizes is so essential.

2 Reportedly, after retiring from Stanford University, F. Terman, the "Godfather of Silicon Valley," tried to leverage his experience as a consultant to countries that were trying to replicate Silicon Valley. But he failed to create a successful case due to not recognizing the existence of US specific "New Capital I" institutions and military R&D facilitating schemes (Kenney, Martin, eds., *Understanding Silicon Valley*, Stanford University Press, 2000).

References

Atkinson, R. D., M. Muro & J. Whiton (2019). *The Case for Growth Centers*. Washington, DC: Brookings Institution and ITIF.

Cavallo, A., A. Ghezzi & R. Balocco (2018). "Entrepreneurial Ecosystem Research: Present Debates and Future Directions," *International Entrepreneurship and Management Journal*, 15(4), 1–43.

Doss, H. & A. Brett (2015). *The Rainforest Scorecard: A Practical Framework for Growing Innovation Potential*. Los Altos, CA: Reganwald.

Feld, B. (2012). *Startup Communities: Building an Entrepreneurial Ecosystem in Your City*. Hoboken, NJ: John Wiley & Sons.

Foss, L. & D. V. Gibson (Eds.) (2015). *The Entrepreneurial University: Context and Institutional Change*. London, UK: Routledge.

Fuentelsaz, L., J. P. Maícas & P. Mata (2018). "Institutional Dynamism in Entrepreneurial Ecosystems" in A. O'Connor et al. (Eds.), *Entrepreneurial Ecosystems: Place-based Transformations and Transitions* (pp. 45–63). New York: Springer.

Haskel, J. & S. Westlake (2022). *Restarting the Future: How to Fix the Intangible Economy*. Princeton, NJ: Princeton University Press.

Mazzucato, M., (2014). *The Entrepreneurial State*. London: Anthem Press.

Mccloskey, D. N., & Mingardi, A., (2020). *The Myth of the Entrepreneurial State*. Great Barrington, MA: The American Institute for Economic Research.

North, D. C. (1990). *Institutions, Institutional Change and Economic Performance*. Cambridge, UK: Cambridge University Press.

O'Connor, Stam, E., Sussan, F. & Audretsch eds. (2018). *Entrepreneurial Ecosystems*. Cham: Springer International Publishing.

Scott, R. W. (2014). *Institutions and Organizations*, 4th Edition. Thousand Oaks, CA: Sage.

Storper, M. (2013). *Keys to the City*. Princeton, NJ: Princeton University Press.

Epilogue from Tsuruoka, Japan

According to the International Institute for Management Development (IMD)'s *World Competitiveness Yearbook 2024*, Japan's industrial competitiveness ranks 38th in the world, the lowest ever recorded. After relinquishing the No. 1 position to the United States in 1993, Japanese industrial competitiveness, which had hovered around the 20th place from the mid-1990s until the 2010s, dropped to the 30s in the 2020s without showing any indication of moving up. The reason for these downgrades can be attributed to Japan's failure to transform its industrial structure from Fordist-style mass-manufacturing-oriented industries to high-tech industries in response to the technological historic paradigm shift from analogue to digital technology.

The collapse of the bubble economy at the end of the 1980s coincided with the end of *the Showa Era* (a period of miraculous high economic growth from the ashes of World War II). The Japanese government, fearing a financial crisis, placed the highest priority on disposing the banks' nonperforming assets in the 1990s—without introducing new policy aimed at the formation of high-tech industries based on digital technology, which would have required drastic structural reforms. As a result, Japan's industrial competitiveness suffered severely, evoking a prolonged economic slump known as the "Lost Decade," an iconic alias of the 1990s. And it continues to this day, resulting in the "Lost Three Decades."

During this long economic stagnation, most Japanese politicians, bureaucrats, and big businesses' managers feared losing the vested status which they had accumulated in the institutions built during the high economic growth period of *the Showa Era*. This fear motivated widespread resistance to the "Political Creative Destruction" that might be brought by structural transformations (Acemoglu et al., 2019). In fact, Tsuru et al. (2019, p. 226) pointed out that the "Structural Reform" emphasized in the Koizumi administration (2001–2006) "became politically evasive" in subsequent administrations in trying to avoid strong rejection from the electorate. As a result, we can conclude that Japan could not facilitate economic growth through strengthening industrial competitiveness (as was being accomplished in the United States) because of this reluctance to promote structural change from existing institutions to new ones.

DOI: 10.4324/9781003488149-7

However, I do hope that the case of Tsuruoka, recognized as one of the successful examples of regional innovation by *The White Paper on Science, Technology, and Innovation 2023* published by the Ministry of Education, Culture, Sports, Science and Technology (MEXT), can serve Japan as a viable model for launching endogenous tech-based economic growth. Tsuruoka should not be regarded as a contingent exceptional case for the revitalization of Japan's regional economies. Rather, applying Austin's case as a yardstick, the case of Tsuruoka shares a common rationale with Austin's success, based on our comparative research as described in this book. Like Austin, the necessary and sufficient condition for Tsuruoka's success can be attributed to "Influencers" who played critical roles in providing a clear vision with unwavering consistency for more than 10 years, inducing regional support of experts and practitioners who could share and overcome the high risks associated with Technology Venturing.

It is admittedly difficult to accomplish this task across Japanese regions, given the dense gravitational pull (a "black hole" if you will want to use) of all resources to Tokyo, including talent—to the existing institutions that enabled the high economic growth in *the Showa Era*. While keeping the status quo can be unacceptable during global and historic technological paradigm shift, this can perhaps be considered the root cause of Japan's industrial competitiveness declining to the 35th place and the prolonged recession known as the "Lost Three Decades."

I would encourage Japan's regions to transform their research universities into entrepreneurial universities and to support tech-based startups through building "New Small i" institutions required for realizing Technology Venturing (Nishizawa, 2023). It's my great pleasure to clarify that the case of Tsuruoka—analyzed in this book using Austin's success as an analytical yardstick—can serve as both a theoretical and a practical model to achieve endogenous tech-based regional economic growth in response to the technological historic paradigm shift in the 21st century in Japan.

Tohoku University
New Industry Creation Hatchery Center (NICHe)
Senior Research Fellow
Akio Nishizawa

References

Acemoglu, D., D. Laibson & J. List (2019). *Economics*, 2nd Edition. London, UK: Peason Education Inc.

IMD World Competitiveness Center (2024). *World Competitiveness Yearbook 2024*, Lausanne, Switzerland, IMD.

MEXT (2023). *The White Paper on Science, Technology, and Innovation 2023*, Tokyo: MEXT.

Nishizawa, A. (2023). "'New Capitalism' and the University Startups (in Japanese)," *VEC Yearbook 2023* (pp. 136–151), Tokyo: Venture Enterprise Center.

Tsuru, K. et al. (2019). *Macro Analysis of Japanese Economy* (in Japanese). Tokyo: Nihon Keizai Shinbun Shupansha.

Acknowledgments

From A. Nishizawa

I would like to thank my many colleagues and friends who supported the publication of this book. Most importantly, I would like to thank my co-researcher and co-author, Dr. Gibson, who provided valuable advice on theoretical analysis as well as profound knowledge of Austin's tech-based economic growth. I am grateful for his friendship shown to me over the past 20 years and for his arranging the precious opportunity to meet with a legendary authority on institutional theory, W. Richard Scott, Professor of Sociology Emeritus, Stanford University. Professor Scott's advice and research publications provided me and Dr. Gibson with an important theoretical basis of our comparative study on Austin and Tsuruoka. In addition, I would like to recognize the late Professor George Kozmetsky who emphasized the need for courage in research and practice. Finally, I would also like to express my gratitude to Margaret Cotrofeld, a talented former administrative assistant at the IC² Institute for her excellent editing of this book's text and graphics, which, given my poor English, made it a little more readable.

From D. Gibson

I would like to thank the IC² Institute, the University of Texas at Austin (UT Austin), for providing me the opportunity and institutional home, for 30+ years, to teach, conduct research, and work with and learn from colleagues and students and Visiting Scholars from a broad range of academic and professional backgrounds representing many US regions and many countries. I especially thank my many mentors and friends at UT Austin and IC² Institute—most importantly, George Kozmetsky—who participated in and helped guide and inform my research and teaching. My collaborations have resulted in a broad range of national and international research projects, professional conferences, published books and research articles, and they also have led to long-lasting friendships. Most recently I appreciate the opportunity to be able to collaborate with and become friends with Professor Akio Nishizawa over the past years as we researched, discussed, and wrote about our comparative research on regional-based economic development. Finally, I thank Margaret Cotrofeld, my administrative and editorial assistant at the IC^2 Institute, who, over many years, provided me with valuable support and advice improving my academic contributions overall and especially my publications.

From Both

Additionally, both authors thank Dr. Colin Mason, Honorary Senior Research Fellow of Adam Smith Business School at the University of Glasgow; Sheridan Tatsuno, Principal, Dreamscape Global; and Dr. Fred Phillips, President of TANDO Institute for reviewing early drafts of our publication and providing useful edits. Finally, we thank Kristina Abbotts, Senior Editor, *Economics, Finance and Accounting*, and Christiana Mandizha, Editorial Assistant, *Economics*, Routledge, and the reviewers of our book proposal for providing useful suggestions and advice.

Index

Note: **Bold** page numbers refer to tables; *italic* page numbers refer to figures and page numbers followed by "n" denote endnotes.